"In the past, I have found Human Design to be complex and confusing. Robin Winn has written a book that is engaging and accessible. It breaks a very complex system into a usable format that is easy to comprehend and puts the framework of understanding immediately to use. The insights provided are helpful not just to the therapist or coach but to anyone working with people. In reading the text, you will find deeper understanding not only of others but of yourself. Highly recommended read!"

— **Stephanie Brill**, founder and board chair of Gender Spectrum, author of *The Transgender Child* and *The Transgender Teen*

"I love it! Very digestible, easy to read, and user-friendly! This book is an excellent resource for therapists looking to understand their clients on a deeper level. With this approach, true healing can take place."

— **Dr. Amanda E. Eller,** physical therapist

"Just reading the Manifestor chapter, and it's great! Really helpful, clear, great insights, nice balance of the positive and more challenging aspects! Knowing two Manifestors very well, it's super accurate and helpful. I can see how incredibly beneficial this book will be in working with my clients, offering me insight about them, and guidance in the best ways to support them in their transformation and healing!"

– **Lucia Maya**, Reiki master and transformational coach

"Robin Winn's book *Understanding Your Clients through Human Design* is brilliant. She distills the essence of this complicated system and makes it a must if one wants to help their clients understand themselves for transformation and healing. My personal sessions with Robin have been extraordinary, and my work with clients has been greatly enhanced following Human Design sessions with her."

– **Jane Bell**, spiritual teacher, guide, mentor, and founder of Presence of Heart

"Robin Winn has written an essential tool for building and inspiring "people leaders." *Understanding Your Clients through Human Design* is the perfect resource for anyone needing to better understand colleagues and "team members" in corporate and non-profit organizations."

– **Arina Isaacson**, International Executive Business Coach, professional faculty, Leadership and Communication, UC Berkeley/Haas School of Business

"With this beautiful book, Robin Winn shares her incredible wealth of knowledge and wisdom making it available and accessible for both clinicians and anyone who is on an evolutionary path."

– Dr. Pearlyn Goodman-Herrick,
naturopathic physician, adjunct professor of homeopathy at the Southwest College of Naturopathic Medicine

"It is well written and perfect for coaches! The energy of the book is magical."

– Mary Murphy, plant medicine integration coach

"*Understanding Your Clients through Human Design* is an eye-opener, elevating your "understanding, compassion, and expansion of who your clients are." I ran charts on my lover and best friend, realizing how powerful this lesson in communication can be for my personal life. Incorporating it professionally must be tremendously effective."

– Ana-Maria Figueredo, author of
The Secret Art of Selling Insurance

"Robin Winn takes very complex information and makes it easy to understand and use. As a CEO, I see this being a tool that I can use daily with my team and that it will help me amplify my leadership ability. Thank you for bringing Human Design into a glidepath that allows leaders and coaches to bring it to our clients and teams so that transformation can be accelerated."

– Tammy Green, CEO,
Anchorage Neighborhood Health Center

"I've been curious about Human Design as a tool to understand myself for years, but not until I read Robin Winn's book did it come together. It's complex but so elegant, and now I can't wait to go further into exploring the layers of this system. As a lifelong educator, I applaud Robin for the clear, humble way she has laid out the pearls of Human Design."

— **Sandy Wallenstein**, EDD K-12, university educator, CEO, GreenUp Learning (www.greenuplearning.com)

"Robin Winn's passion and appreciation for Human Design infuses these pages. Like an MRI for the soul, Human Design helps coaches and therapists see inside their client's personal operating systems. As someone who helps people identify their calling and purpose in life, I find Human Design to be an incredible tool for understanding how each person fits in to the wider puzzle of humanity. We each have a calling and a role to play; Robin Winn helps practitioners who are brand new to Human Design get their feet wet with this complex and fascinating system. If you work with clients and are interested in acquiring a new diagnostic tool, I recommend reading *Understanding Your Clients through Human Design*, cover to cover!"

— **The Rev. Dr. Sara Shisler Goff**, best-selling author of *The Art of Feminine Spiritual Leadership*

"I *love* this book! Robin is succinct, clear, and vibrantly intimate in the transmission of her writing *Understanding Your Clients through Human Design*. After thirty years as a therapist and clinical supervisor in community mental health agencies, I transitioned to private practice just as Robin's book was coming out. I decided to work with her to incorporate Human Design into my work with my clients. What has transpired is truly amazing. My clients are nodding, eyes wide, as I describe to them their specific type and the strategies which help them navigate through life. This knowledge is transforming my work and my clients!"

– Heidi Winn, LMHC

"When Robin says 'the breakthrough technology for serving your clients,' she is absolutely spot on. The amazing bonus is this book will not only serve your clients, it will also serve your family and, most importantly, yourself. Her practical, down-to-earth voice and her take on the information presented has been invaluable in my day-to-day living and has helped so many people in my life and work."

– Charity Hyams, author of *The Widow's Survival Guide*, widow coach, speaker, and mother of three

"*Understanding Your Clients through Human Design* has changed my life personally, and I am very much looking forward to using it professionally. Winn teaches the basics of Human Design in a very easy-to-understand way, which is key since the original writings are very complicated. I highly recommend reading this book to get a better understanding of yourself and to get an incredible new tool to better understand the puzzle pieces of your clients so you can help them achieve better results, faster."

– **Lyndsay Toensing,** MBA, author of
The Art of Connected Leadership, speaker,
transformational leadership coach and consultant

"Knowing my own Human Design has allowed me to soar in my life and career. This information has completely changed how I show up in the world and magnetize my life purpose to be able to help more people quicker. After reading Robin Winn's book, I am able to artfully use Human Design as well as other energetic tools to guide my patients & physician clients from burnout and skepticism to healing and happiness."

– **Veronica Anderson**, MD, author of *Too Smart to Be
Struggling: The Guide for Over-Scheduled Doctors to
Find Happiness (and Make More Money, Too)*

"Robin Winn's book is fantastic – it invites everyone to value their design and to delight in the diversity of who we each are which is what connects us. I look forward to reading it again and highly recommend it for all therapists, coaches, and care-givers of any sort. Through Robin's support and the guidance in her book, I understand myself in a new way and feel more able to effectively support, as well as understand, not only my students and clients, but also my family, friends and partner."

– **Clare McLaughlin**, licensed psychotherapist, human development curriculum innovator, Path of Essence teacher

"This book brings the powerful technology of Human Design immediately into your practice. It makes available informa-tion that shines a bright light on the innate, unique pattern of each client and their optimal way of function and expres-sion. It empowers the therapy and coaching, shaping it spe-cifically to each client's design. This book is a game changer for every coach and therapist."

– **Pali Summerlin**, spiritual teacher, consciousness coach

"Robin Winn is able to take a multi-faceted, complex system of information and communicate it clearly in a way that it makes sense and is useful. As a result it is a game changer in people's lives."

– **David Groode**, professional psychic

"When you understand the particulars of your Human Design, you begin living in right alignment with who you are. Robin Winn does a superb job at both unfolding and clarifying the language of the Human Design system. Her descriptions are crisp, her examples are poignant. This is not only an insightful book for therapists and coaches but for anyone interested in gaining a better perspective on how they operate in the world."

– **Gary Bell**, permit expediter, researcher

"I'm *overjoyed* that I found this book when I did. It's like having a sherpas guide with me while working with new clients, it leads to breakthrough moments almost immediately! It's powerfully written and easy to use. That's big when it comes to navigating Human Design work. *Understanding Your Clients through Human Design* is an amazing companion for coaches and therapists when Human Design is in your wheelhouse of support. I consider Robin the number one authority on Human Design for educating coaches, therapists alike. She is amazing resource and I can't wait for book two!"

– **Angelina Lombardo**, bestselling author,
trauma informed coach, and speaker

"Robin Winn has done all of us a great service in writing a clear and concise book teaching helping professionals how to understand our clients through Human Design. Robin's focused view of this complex system makes it accessible to, and relevant for, non-specialists. She reviews and then applies the key aspects of the system to the clients of therapists, coaches, and other transformational practitioners. Full of stories and illuminating examples, Robin's book brings Human Design into the mainstream – where it belongs!"

– **Maggie Sale Ostara**, PhD, spiritual mentor, educator, speaker, business coach

UNDERSTANDING YOUR CLIENTS THROUGH HUMAN DESIGN

ROBIN WINN, MFT

THE BREAKTHROUGH TECHNOLOGY

Difference Press, Washington, D.C., USA
© Robin Winn, 2020

ISBN: 978-1-68309-274-2

Cover Design: Jennifer Stimson
Interior Book Design: Kozakura
Editing: Moriah Howell
Author Photo Credit: Juliet Jarmosco

DP

DIFFERENCE
PRESS

For all the Wise Guides who consistently appear precisely when I need them, and who perfectly and compassionately point the way.

May these words honor you.

TABLE OF CONTENTS

SECTION 3: WORKING WITH CLIENTS – HUMAN DESIGN IN ACTION

SECTION 4: GOING FORWARD

Chapter 14

I have always believed that the potential to use Human Design as a powerful therapeutic tool has been largely untapped since the creation of this life-changing system in 1987.

Human Design, a synthesis of Eastern and Western Astrology, the Chinese I Ching, the Hindu Chakra system and Judaic Kabbalah is a cross-cultural system of using archetypes to get to the root of why and how people cultivate meaning in their lives.

Any new modality has to struggle in order to demonstrate its efficacy and validity. Human Design has been waiting for someone like Robin Winn, to take this system and make it accessible as a ground-breaking, therapeutic tool to help people get to the root cause of pain in their lives and to see the potential of possibility in crafting a new, more empowered personal narrative.

As a nurse and a coach, I've always seen the value of using Human Design in conjunction with the work I do with my clients. In the twenty years that I've been using and teaching

Human Design I've seen this powerful system dramatically shorten the length of time a person needs to create radical transformation in their lives.

The stories we tell about who we are and the beliefs we have about "how" we are, create the trajectory of our lives. Counseling and therapy offer people a safe way to heal and to navigate the path to crafting a new, more authentic personal narrative.

Human Design, as a tool, offers people a "map," a way through the journey of redefining themselves as more whole, more resilient and more empowered. Robin has taken her deep knowledge of this system and given practitioners a template to support clients through this journey of transformation.

Human Design gives people a simple vocabulary to help them find the words to explain those subtle and indefinable places where they feel that there is "more" to who they are but they can't express it. It verifies what people often hope is true about themselves, that "secret" part of the inner terrain of their heart, that they want to share with the world, but they often don't have the tools or the language to express.

The power of this language became clear to me after giving a seventy-five-year old-woman her first Human Design reading. She cried off and on during the one hour we spent together, and shared with me at the end of her session that she felt "seen" for the first time in her life.

No one should have to wait seventy-five years to feel "seen."

What Robin gives practitioners in this book is a fast and powerful way to make people feel "seen" and for them to find the beauty and the power of who they are using the language and the story of their Human Design.

Robin shows how practitioners can use Human Design to help their clients confirm what they had always hoped was true about themselves – to give them the words to tell a more authentic personal narrative – and strategies to activate deeper states of healing and high performance.

Human Design is a complementary system that gives practitioners deeper insights that go beyond cognitive therapy. Not only is Human Design a cross-cultural index of personality archetypes, it's also a powerful way to support clients in understanding their strengths, their gifts and why they may be predisposed to certain challenges.

Human Design gives us a new way to reframe many complex psychological concepts like self-sabotage, projection, co-dependency, empathy and more. What Human Design shows us is that we are affected by the world in unique ways that go beyond our imprinting, conditioning and experiences. We are uniquely configured to experience the world in a way that can often be easily explained by Human Design. While this awareness will never replace therapy or coaching, it does give the practitioner a powerful starting point to begin the process of helping clients self-actualize with love.

Our Human Design contains the code for our life curriculum and teaches us what we need to master in order to cultivate our maturity, our purpose and our wisdom. The process of personal growth takes place over time, through experience. Human Design helps clients master the cycles of their life and the stages of growth that lead to maturity and fulfillment.

I have found over the years that when people don't live true to who they are, when they try to be something they're not and when they hold themselves back from the full expression of the unique story that only they can live, they experience pain in every area of their lives.

Not only that, the amount of energy that it takes to maintain a mask or a facade, is depleting eventually leading to burnout. People who are burned out have elevated levels of cortisol leading to a whole host of physical challenges and even depression, which, according to the World Health Organization occupies first place in the global disease burden of the world.

Robin's profound professional and spiritual understandings and her rich knowledge of how to blend Human Design with coaching and therapeutic systems, helps you guide your clients in a rich, practical way through the journey of activating not only their life purpose, but offers them a concrete strategy to live a more authentic life and access greater level of well-being.

This book promises to add a powerful dimension to your work with clients, gives you a strong and accurate starting point to get to the root cause of your client's pain, enables you to help your clients tap into higher levels of performance and, ultimately, shows you practical ways to enhance your client's wellness and deepen the meaning of their lives.

Karen Curry Parker, B.S.N, CFC
#1 Bestselling author of *Understanding Human Design*, *Human Design Activation Guide*, and *Abundance by Design*
Creator of The Quantum Alignment System.
Renowned Leader, Speaker, Mentor, and Teacher of Human Design as a Catalytic Conversation

Section 1

INTRODUCTION

CHAPTER 1

SERVING YOUR CLIENTS – BREAKTHROUGHS IN YOUR WORK

Two years ago, I was giving a Human Design session to a well-known and highly successful therapist. As we looked at her design, she was moved by the accuracy the chart reflected. She said that I was articulating things that she intuitively knew, but that had never been put into words. She suddenly had language for what made her so different. It was deeply affirming and nourishing for her, supportive of who she was and the work she was doing. She was surprised at the grounded guidance the chart showed about how to best use her energy and had a new understanding regarding the projections she was getting.

At one point, she looked up at me and said, "I think this would be really helpful for a client of mine. We've been doing incredible work and have hit a pocket where I'm not sure of the best way forward. Knowing her chart could help us." We did eventually look at the client's chart, and it did bring a breakthrough that helped shift the work to a new place. Ever since then, this therapist always gets the Human Design chart of any new clients she takes on. She understands the value of having the information and the impact it has on her work. In the beginning, she would consult with me about the charts, and now she has enough information, for the most part, to work with them herself.

It dawned on me that every therapist, and every coach for that matter, needed to know this tool was available for them. Anyone in the transformational field who is looking to contribute to people's lives and wants to know a better way to support their clients would benefit from using Human Design in their work. I wondered how could I bring this relatively new technology into the mainstream.

In the past year, I participated in two coaching programs: one called Transformational Speaking, the other The Author Incubator (out of which I wrote this book). Both were fantastic programs. In both cases, I was part of a group, being coached myself, and witnessing people being coached. I saw over and over how much easier it would have been for everyone if the coaches had known the participant's design – how much more skillfully they could have supported us.

As coaches and therapists, we like it when we can help our clients understand themselves. When our clients can zoom out and have perspective on themselves and their lives, it changes how they treat themselves and how they operate in the world.

It's deeply rewarding to see people shift from a negative, no-possibility view of themselves and their world into a compassionate, empowered vantage. From these new lenses, they can begin forging paths to a richer life. Not only are our clients empowered, we feel like we're on purpose in our work.

But sometimes it's not so easy to make sense of what's going on with a person. It's then that our work becomes much more challenging. Perhaps it is a particular behavior that's difficult for us, or a developmental stage, or a client's seeming inability to take responsibility for their lives. We hit these pockets where we get stuck. It's hard. We don't like the feeling of helplessness – in our clients or ourselves. We prefer being in the flow or the zone with our clients. And we like it when they are too! We aspire to loving our work, feeling like we're making a difference. Those times we feel bogged down, unsure of ourselves, inadequate, or in a haze are challenging and difficult.

Maybe you're a successful therapist or coach who loves supporting people in being successful in their lives. Maybe you work with individuals or couples in recovery to help them work through trauma. You're good at what you do. Your toolbox serves you well. You're smart. You're capable. You trust yourself and your work. Yet, when you hit those eddies with your clients where you just can't figure out how to work with someone, you're motivated to see what else might help you understand and better support your client. The feeling of lack creates an opening to try something new.

Imagine for a moment that you have a powerful, cutting edge diagnostic system that gives you immediate insight into your client and empowers your work – not only for the challenging clients but for all your clients. Imagine that you have a window into their world that will help you help them get the perspective they need to move out of a victimized, pathologized, limited view of themselves and move into compassion and understanding for themselves. What if you could, in a non-biased way, reflect their challenges, their strengths, their optimal way of navigating in the world?

Would you want that? Of course you would!

When my father, a surgeon, went to his yearly cardiovascular meetings to get the latest in surgery techniques, he looked forward to having cutting-edge knowledge to increase his diagnostic capacity and skill set to make his work more effective for his patients and to improve the outcomes for them in surgery.

If you're picking up this book you have either had a Human Design session that was life-changing for you, you've heard about someone else who has had transformational shift from learning their design, you know of a therapist or coach who is using Human Design in their work, or something about Human Design resonates with you – you may not even know what.

Human Design is here for you to help serve your clients at the highest level. It's here to help you understand yourself as a practitioner and to help you support your clients on their path. Having this knowledge increases your capacity to provide results. I guarantee that. A tool of differentiation, Human Design helps you make sense out of nonsense, clear the fog, and approach your work with more confidence and a lighter step.

As you read this book, you will gain access to the first level of Human Design: Type, Strategy, and Authority. This is the most basic and potent information in the Human Design system. Knowing this fundamental level will instantly change how you approach your clients. The first step is to understand and master this basic level. Once that is achieved, you will most likely want to explore the highly complex, multiple layered information available from the chart including: inherent vulnerabilities and strengths, learning styles, life purpose, what drives your clients, where they in are the life cycle, what are their biggest gifts, what is their spiritual path, what are their conundrums, how they relate to others, and so on.

As you master more and more of the foundational understanding, your ease with the information will increase, and your capacity to see and support your clients will expand, taking your work to an unforeseen level of expertise, potency, and ease.

CHAPTER 2

THE JOURNEY OF DIFFERENTIATION

As I mentioned in chapter 1, my dad was a cardiovascular surgeon. Every year, he and my mom would take us to some fancy resort around the country – Colorado and Hawaii stand out as memorable – and we would go to the beach or hike while he attended meetings. It was a given that education was important in our family and that these yearly meetings he attended, as well as the continuous stream of medical journals he devoured, were crucial to his competency as an MD.

The drive for excellence and competency in the name of serving at the highest level was embedded into the fabric of my being. Likewise, having a professional career was the expectation for me and my six siblings. I started as somewhat of a disappointment in that regard. After graduating from UC Berkeley in English, I meandered for a few years: I interned with Phyllis Chester on her book *Mothers On Trial*, worked at East West Books in NYC, taught yoga, housecleaned, and cared for infants and toddlers at The Duck Pond in the Berke-ley Hills. It wasn't until I was twenty-five that I embarked on my "career" as a Rosen Method Bodywork Practitioner. As far as my parents were concerned, this was better than childcare and housecleaning but not in the ballpark of what they imag-ined and hoped for me.

What they couldn't envision was that Rosen Work would become a recognized, well-respected, leading form of transfor-mational bodywork world-wide. Marion Rosen, a Mayo-Clinic trained physical therapist who had fled Nazi Germany, discov-ered that people got better faster when they talked while she worked with them. She was teaching her students to access the unconscious through body tension and breath, through aware-ness and relaxation. Her work formed my foundational under-standing of how to listen and hold space for the possibility of who people are beneath their defensive body tensions. Our Rosen brochures quoted Marion, saying, "This work is about transformation – from the person we think we are to the per-son we really are. In the end, we can't be anyone else." This seed became my organizing principle, my guiding light for all the educational paths that I was to follow.

After creating a successful Rosen practice, focusing on working with sexual abuse survivors, it became clear that I needed more ground to meet my clients' emotional struggles. I got tired of people connecting deeply to their core wounds on my table, then having to send them to therapy to work with what had surfaced. I wanted to be doing the next phase of work with them. I began graduate work in Somatic Psychology, though I ultimately got my master's degree in the new field of Feminist Psychology.

Being steeped in an alternative lifestyle and adverse to the medical model, I had a love/hate relationship with the DSM (Diagnostic and Statistical Manual). Always one intrigued by systems, I felt the pathologizing of people, while initially helpful in some cases and sometimes important, was in many cases dismissive and underestimated people's capacities. I struggled through my resistance to finish my degree and get my 3,000 internship hours. Fortunately, I had supervisors who were brilliant and innovative, helping me discern what was old school and what rules could be modified to engage a more relational model that would best serve the client.

In 1997, I met Byron Katie and was given my next breakthrough toolset. The Work was an invitation to look at thoughts, inquire into their truth, and ultimately discover what was truer. This simple system and my close relationship with Katie radically transformed my perspective on my childhood story and dramatically changed how I worked with clients. Acting as a therapist, I had empathized with my clients' nightmare stories, supported their entitlement to feeling like victims, and gently nourished them to a self-loving embrace. Katie's work cut the victim story out and went for liberation – life beyond the story. It was spiritual cognitive therapy on steroids. I couldn't get enough of it. Attending Katie's first school, traveling around the US and Europe on staff as her curriculum coordinator for The School for The Work, I was bathed in the clarity of her radical teachings. And, of course, I brought The Work to my clients who experienced, as I had, another level of empowerment and a deeper knowing of the Truth of who they were.

Meeting Faisal Muqaddam and being introduced to The Diamond Logos Approach added another dimension to my understanding of myself and my work with my clients. A combination of Eastern mysticism and Western psychology, The Diamond Logos Work provided a comprehensive map of the journey from living an ego-based life to living embodied in Beingness. Shifting from Human Doing to true Human Being. This work relied on self-inquiry, a deep understanding of the Enneagram, and the understanding and transmission of various essential qualities that were lost as we separated from our essential self to identify with our ego. I ultimately became a teacher of Diamond Logos in this powerful and profound journey of meeting the Self. It was in the teacher training that I was first introduced to Human Design by a colleague, but I'll hold off on that story for a moment.

As you can see, my work with clients began through the access portal of the body, then shifted to exploring the emotional self, the mental constructs, ultimately using an understanding of the Enneagram and the nourishment of transmissions of essence to differentiate and navigate the mistaken ego identity that keeps us from who we truly are. Through the Diamond Work, I was introduced to Lama Palden and her Kagyu Shangpa Lineage of Tibetan Buddhism. I added this extraordinary path, and her dakini-infused guidance, into the mix and began what is now a fifteen-year, in-depth practice of Vajrayana Buddhism. These teachings, elaborate and profound, brought an exquisite articulation of suffering, the causes of suffering, and the pathways out of suffering, leading to True Nature, the marriage of the relative and the absolute. The Buddhist version of Marion Rosen's teaching: suffering comes from mistaken identity.

In 2004, I was brought to my knees when, following the first rain of the fall, a car swerved on the slippery road into my BMW as I drove on the Marin freeway to see Lama Palden for my Diamond session. As often happens, these travesties are doorways to the next opportunity, and the debilitating concussion I incurred led me to the next cutting-edge tools that would again transform my life and my work with clients.

This time there were two technologies that, through my healing, diversified and upgraded how I approached the journey from limitation to possibility. The first began with an Anat Baniel session that led me to taking the Anat Baniel Method Training. This NeuroMovement practice utilizes gentle movement to access the brain to perceive differences and re-pattern our neurotransmitter pathways. Here, I again discovered that things were not as they appeared. I witnessed miracle after miracle. As an example, one woman who hadn't raised her arm in twenty years had a full range of motion after a single movement lesson. I learned to move slowly with attention in a variety of ways, acutely perceiving differences. As I did, my brain function upgraded, my body pain dissipated, and I started de-aging. Who would have thought?

Parallel to Anat's work, I began intensive study with Ming Tong Gu in Wisdom Healing Qigong. This tradition was born at the largest medicine-less hospital in China where people came from all over to heal their incurable ailments, from cancer to diabetes to heart disease. It was during Ming Tong's first Healing Intensive in Sebastopol, California that I had the visceral experience of not being able to solve the problem at the level of the problem. At that point, my brain was not healing. I could not tolerate sound, light, or input. Following a Lift Chi Up Pour Chi Down practice where I had felt my body expand to fill the entire universe, I lay on the ground and had the experience of my consciousness expanding beyond my brain, and the excruciating pain that it held. I experienced myself as bigger than the pain. I was freed from believing my identification with my mind/brain. There was peace. It's hard to describe, but I will never forget that liberation in the face of locked-in, helpless terror.

Just before the car accident, I had my first Human Design session. I mentioned earlier that I was initially introduced to Human Design by a colleague in the Diamond Teachers'

Training. I had been hearing Kamud talk about it, I knew I wanted to do it, but it took me almost a year before I made the appointment. I remember sitting at the computer with Kamud as she acknowledged that it was perfect that I waited, that I was not designed to make hasty or spontaneous decisions (more about this in chapter 12). There is not a lot I remember about that first session; mostly, it felt very obscure and esoteric, hard to comprehend. The big takeaway for me was the understanding that I was a Generator and needed to follow my Sacral *yeses* and *nos*. I had access to energy and was designed to work.

Following this inner *yes* was something that I was familiar with. My partner Yarrow had tried to get me to move from our house in Berkeley to Marin. I had a clear *no*. I didn't want to sell our home that was five minutes from our office. I didn't want to rent. I didn't want to commute. I couldn't see how it was possible. Something in me was not going to budge. It was a body response. Initially, I humored Yarrow and went along for the adventure as she took me to open house after open house. She was inviting me into a dream and I entered the fantasy. At some point, I couldn't even do that. I refused. I drew the line. Yarrow was left to explore the dream on her own. For two years, she followed Craigslist ads, asking me from time to time if I would go look at a home. The answer was always *no*. On September 16, 2004, we were heading to Point Reyes with our friends Char and Lynn to celebrate Char's birthday with a hike to the ocean. Yarrow said there was a house for rent on the way, and asked if we could just stop by to see it. The people wouldn't be home, she promised. We could just look. I somewhat reluctantly agreed, as long as it was okay with Char and Lynn.

As we made our way toward the little town of Inverness, Yarrow took a left up Dream Farm Road. Something in me started to wake up. Already, my inner GPS was responding to the name of the road. It was as if I had entered a magical world. Meandering through the forest up to the house my whole body was screaming *yes*. Turns out the woman who was moving out was home, and we knew her. We were all students of Leslie Temple Thurston, another beloved spiritual teacher. The house was a creative vortex, filled with Kathleen's art, like a verdant garden blossoming throughout the house. My *no* became a full-on *yes*. It was a done deal. By Thanksgiving, we had sold our home of fifteen years and moved to Inverness.

I could never have imagined moving from Berkeley to that magical, nature-drenched world. My brain couldn't conceive of it, but as I reflected on my Human Design reading, I realized that the Sacral response was the mechanism that guided me. As I looked back over my life, I could see where I had made seemingly illogical decisions in the same way and that each one had opened doorways to unforeseen possibilities. I could also see where I made decisions from my head that had led me to dead ends. Having this Generator inner GPS mechanism articulated made me appreciate and validate my decision-making strategy and to use it consciously.

The other huge and life-changing piece of information I got from the session was about my relationship with Yarrow. As it turns out, while I am a Generator, Yarrow is a Projector. We had been together twenty-three years at the time of the reading. Our relationship had been a major growth experience for both of us. We had invested years in couple's therapy, learning good communication skills and deepening our understanding of each other. We'd written volumes of The Work on each other, bravely and fiercely judging each other to discover more about ourselves. We had deep love, but we were essentially different – and were daily bumping up against those differences. With all my efforts to accept her, I still fundamentally wanted her to be different. I basically couldn't understand why she needed so much rest and downtime. I perceived that as lazy. She, meanwhile, could not comprehend why I worked so much. She valued that spacious silence of being and wanted me to be with her in that. She wanted me to linger in bed and enjoy the ease. She thought I was a workaholic.

When I heard Kamud say that Yarrow, as a Projector, is not designed to work, that she is a wise guide here to support Generators and that she gets exhausted from all the Generator energy and needs more rest... well, as you can imagine, my world turned. The light went on and I saw how I had been judging our differences rather than valuing them. This began a process that continues to this day of opening to her contribution as a Projector. Not only did this Human Design information organize our relationship at a higher level, bringing more space, aliveness, and respect, but it also, as I later began studying Human Design, massively helped me understand, support, and work with my Projector clients.

Like Ra, the original recipient of Human Design, my immersion into Human Design began with a transmission of the system. In 2013, Yarrow and I had recently moved from Point Reyes to Iowa, and I had just flown back to the Bay Area to see clients and visit friends. I was staying with my soul-friends Jane and Gary Bell at their home, which overlooked Tomales Bay. Sitting on their coffee table next to books on Egypt was a red book: *Understanding Human Design* by Karen Curry (now Karen Parker). I picked up the book and immediately that *yes* signal started flashing. As I began reading her completely accessible and easily graspable teaching on Human Design, the information started downloading in me. The whole thing made perfect sense. I contacted Karen and began the in-depth study which continues with her to this day.

As I grounded the information, I immediately began running all my friends', family's, and clients' charts. *Oh, this client is a Projector. Oh, this one is a Manifestor.* Suddenly, I understood my mother who was a Manifestor. And after twenty years as a psychotherapist, my work with clients came into a new focus. Issues that had been consistent made sense. *Oh, you have the Gate of Struggle – you're designed to struggle. That's not wrong, it's just a matter of making sure you pick struggles that are right for you. Then they are gratifying.* The amount of information and clarity was mind-boggling.

It reminded me of sitting at the dinner table as an eighth-grader in 1972 and hearing my dad talk about the new X-ray machines: CT scans. And again as a college freshman, hearing about MRIs and how revolutionary they were, how much more information he could get, and how helpful that was in diagnosing and treating people.

I had a new diagnostic tool.

How I approached myself, my clients, my friends, and my family changed.

How I perceived myself as a practitioner was forever altered. According to my Human Design Incarnation Cross, I'm here to bring something new to humanity, to "transcend all self-imposed or unnecessarily limiting boundaries and make my vision for change available and applicable to everyone..." as stated in *The Book of Destinies* by Chetan Parkyn & Carola Eastwood. My conscious sun in Gate 3 is all about having difficulty at the beginning because I am bringing changes to the world. With my open G (Identity Center), no wonder I've studied so many modalities, always looking for the next path. It wasn't wrong for me to use whatever tool I could find. I wasn't designed to dig one well.

Human Design gave me a new context. A new way of understanding, appreciating, and valuing difference rather than using pathology to separate myself from the "other." Never comfortable with the top-down model of being the "expert," this system gave me a way to work on a level playing field, meeting my clients with respect and curiosity, not identifying them with their problems. I had a way to look at and understand the space within which the conundrums or challenges arose. From that ground, I could offer the tools to help them meet those challenges, without being identified with them. Like having the information from an MRI I began to see what had been there all along but didn't have differentiation capacity to recognize.

In my chart, I'm here to improve the conditions of humanity. Just as the CT scans, MRIs, and laser surgery revolutionized medicine, Human Design is available to expedite our path of understanding ourselves, our relationships, and our clients. I look forward to hearing about your journey of stepping into these waters and discovering for yourself the power and ease of understanding people and working with them that awaits you.

CHAPTER 3

Getting Oriented

If you've tried to enter the world of Human Design and been stymied by the complexity of the language or the system, my intention in this book is to give you easy access. As with any new undertaking, there is a learning curve that requires a level of surrender. Don't let the density of information deter you. Hang with it. When you studied the Myers Briggs or the Enneagram or the DSM, you had to orient yourself, but once you got the structure, you could put it to use. My hope is that you will be able to look at a chart and immediately better understand the person you're working with.

GETTING THE BIG PICTURE: START TO FINISH

I'm someone who is grounded by the big picture. If that is the case for you, then I suggest you read this book chapter by chapter through to the end. Take your time. The material has a transmission to it, so it's not like you can just read it through the portal of your logical left brain! Give yourself time to digest and integrate. Whenever we're learning something new, it's like building muscles at the gym – there's a stress factor involved. I suggest you allow for that.

OVERVIEW

This book is broken into sections. This first section is the introduction. In Section 2, we'll cover the foundation of Human Design; in Section 3, we'll look at putting Human Design into action, and in Section 4, we'll look at what's ahead on this journey.

More specifically, in Section 2: The Fundamentals of Human Design, we begin chapter 4 discovering how Human Design came to be, what it is, how a chart is determined, and the mechanics of the chart. This is the nuts and bolts of Human Design and will cover hexagrams, the planets in the hexagrams, how to transpose the hexagrams onto the chart, the gates, channels, and centers, definition versus openness, and circuitry.

Chapter 5 continues with the nuts and bolts as we look at the Five Human Design Types in general: what they are and how they're determined. You'll also be introduced to Strategy, which accompanies each Type and is key to how each Type best functions.

Section 3: Working with Clients begins with Chapter 6: Getting Started. Here, you enter the practice aspect of Human Design. You'll learn how to get a chart, how to jump into the

Human Design waters, and what to do if the chart doesn't seem to fit. I include a few thoughts about Human Design, suffering, and your client's possible response to their charts.

In chapters 7 through 11, you'll look at how to approach your client depending on their Type. You'll learn about each of the Types: the Generator, the Manifesting Generator, the Manifestor, the Projector, and the Reflector. In these chapters, you'll find the Strategy for each Type, the gifts, challenges, and ways to approach your clients by Type.

Chapter 12 focuses specifically on Authority, which shows the best decision-making strategy for your client.

In Section 4, we'll look at what you might encounter going forward. I'll address challenges with incorporating Human Design in chapter 13.

And, finally, in chapter 14, I speak to the potential of Human Design in creating a paradigm shift in your work.

JUMPING IN: USING THIS BOOK AS A RESOURCE

I've just given you the big picture of this book, but if you're somewhat familiar with Human Design and want to use this book as a resource, you can go straight to the particular Type in chapters 7 to 11 that is indicated on the chart you're looking at. Then, you can look on the chart to see what your client's Authority is and simply go to chapter 12 on Authority.

A Cup of Tea

Regardless of how you use the book, the important thing is that you approach Human Design with a lighthearted, open curiosity and the willingness to undergo an alchemical transformation. When you read this book, you are receiving both a download of information and a practice. As you engage with the material, it wakes up and reveals itself to you.

There is a story we tell in Tibetan Buddhism about approaching the teachings that I think fits here:

Imagine that you are coming to these teachings on Human Design with a teacup. If your cup is full, there is no room for what is offered. If your cup has a crack, then what's offered will leak out. If the cup is dirty, the offering will be tainted. I invite you to read this book with your cup clean and ready to receive the whole of what's offered: the left-brain information, the right brain download, and the transmission of the light beings. Be open to what resonates. Trust yourself. Explore. Play. Discover and know for yourself.

My colleagues, clients, friends, and I have found it amazingly spot-on and supportive. I'm looking forward to hearing how it impacts you, your work, and your clients' lives!

Section 2

The Fundamentals of Human Design

CHAPTER 4

UNDERSTANDING THE CHART

There are many types of profiling systems to help us understand ourselves and our clients. Some involve tests like the Myers Briggs or the Enneagram. Some are self-determined: for example, in Tibetan Buddhism, people often look to see where they land in the Five Buddha Families to understand themselves in terms of their proclivities in awakened activity and ego-centered activity. Then there are systems like astrology that generate information about a person by using birth time, place and date to determine the location of the planets at the time of a person's birth. Human Design falls into this category. It relies on birth information and the placement of our planets to create a bodygraph, a reflection of a person's operating system. With this information, we have a window of understanding into a person's life.

In any of these systems, if you know how to crack the code, there is a wealth of information available. I value systems and find them very useful ... as long as they are kept in perspective. If we get too fixated, the system becomes a label and a box.

It then limits us and our vantage of the people we're working with. I hope that using the system of Human Design will help you open the box and create the opportunity for deeper understanding, compassion, and expansion of who your clients are. It is with the aspiration of elevating our understanding of ourselves and our clients that I share my knowledge and experience of Human Design.

You will find there is a plethora of information that comes from a Human Design chart. It is said that the chart itself carries a transmission, and once someone has seen their chart, a process of transformation is initiated that continues for seven years. During this time, there is an unwinding of the conditioning a person has taken on. When you know your client's chart, you can focus on the areas of vulnerability and support this unwinding process.

It's beyond the scope of this book to present all the levels of information available through the chart. For our purposes, we will focus on Type, Strategy, and Authority. These are the foundational aspects of the chart. If you know and understand these three things, by simply having your client's chart you will have powerful resources to support your work. To understand Type, which is introduced in chapter 5, you'll need to know how we derive the Type. Bear with me while I explain the details of the chart, which, once you understand, will be simple and clear.

THE BASICS

To understand the basic mechanics of Human Design, we begin with how Human Design came into being, and then turn to look at how we determine our design. This involves an introduction to the elements that comprise the Human Design chart:

- The I Ching hexagrams
- The black and red numbers you see on a chart
- How those numbers show up on and create the bodygraph
- Gates
- Channels
- Centers
- Definition
- Circuitry

I know it's a lot to absorb. Take your time with it. If the information doesn't make sense right away, come back to it when you have the bandwidth to take in something new!

THE INCEPTION

The story of Human Design as I know it begins in 1987 off the coast of Spain where a Canadian fellow was on retreat. It was the Harmonic Convergence, and he came back to his cabin to discover it was filled with light beings. They told him that they were going to download a system to help with the evolution of humanity. Ra, as he's now called, known as the reluctant mystic, spent three days receiving the very specific and detailed Human Design download. He was told that the information belonged to everybody, but was particularly important for parents to use in order to understand their children. Inherent in the information is the knowledge that we are each unique and perfectly designed. Humanity is like one big giant puzzle with each person vital to the whole. If someone is trying to live another person's design, then they are not bringing their particular gift to humanity. They are unfulfilled and unhappy, and humanity loses out. If parents can understand their child's design, then the chances of the child living the truth of who they are and offering what they're here to bring increases. If parents are projecting and conditioning their children to be who the parents want or believe they should be, the child runs the risk of spending a lifetime questioning themselves, living a life turned against themselves, and feeling that something is fundamentally wrong with them.

From the Human Design perspective, we are not broken and in need of fixing. We are not problems to be solved. When we know our design, we can skillfully use the energies and the template bestowed at birth for transformation and actualization. When we know and live our design, we can walk in the world unabashedly, embracing our gifts and having compassion for our foibles.

DETERMINING OUR DESIGN

Human Design is a synthesis of astrology, the Judaic Kabbalah, the Chinese I Ching, the Hindu chakra system, and quantum physics.

If you're familiar with astrology, at the time of your birth the planets were in some configuration above and below the horizon, placed within the twelve houses and twelve astrological signs. In Human Design, instead of the planets placed in the houses and signs, they are placed in some combination of the 64 hexagrams of the I Ching. Don't worry about getting all of this right away; the important thing is to get the basic sense of it.

THE I CHING HEXAGRAMS

The I Ching is an ancient system of divination often called The Book of Wisdom. It is comprised of 64 hexagrams. Each hexagram is made of six parallel whole or broken lines. The whole, or solid, lines are yang or masculine. The broken lines are yin or feminine.

The first hexagram is six solid lines, the most yang/masculine expressive energy in the chart:

The second hexagram is six broken lines, the most yin/feminine or receptive energy in Human Design:

The third hexagram is a combination of solid and broken lines, as are the remaining 61 hexagrams:

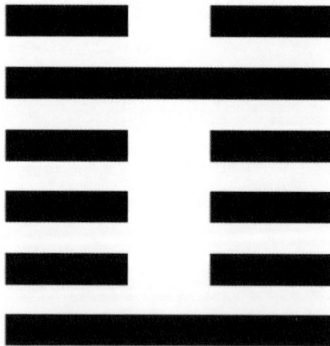

Each hexagram has meaning, containing certain information. The first hexagram, for example, the most yang/masculine energy in the chart, has to do with the strong energy of making a creative contribution. I think of the first hexagram like sperm out to create.

At the time of your client's birth, their planets were in some combination of those 64 hexagrams. If your client has their sun in the first hexagram, you can imagine that a big part of their life revolves around the theme of making or attempting to make a creative contribution. While it's important to understand the aspects of the chart, the study of the hexagrams and their meanings in combination with the planets is more advanced. While I will touch on it here if you'd like more information I suggest you look at Karen Curry's user-friendly book, *Understanding Human Design.*

THE BODYGRAPH: THE BLACK NUMBERS

When you look at a chart you will see two sets of numbers: the set on the right is black and the set on the left is red. At the time of your birth, the neutrino stream (this is the quantum physics part of Human Design) picked up the energies of the planets and the information of the hexagrams they occupied. The black numbers indicate which hexagrams your planets were in at the time of your birth.

These black numbers are sometimes referred to as *the mind, the soul, the personality*, or *the conscious* aspect.

Because the information in black is conscious, when you point out these qualities to your client they will most likely recognize them and identify with them. In the chart below, you'll see the black number 41 at the top of the line of numbers next to a symbol of the sun. This indicates that at the time of birth, this person's sun was occupying the 41st hexagram. Hexagram 41, or, as we say in Human Design, Gate 41, holds the energy of imagining what's possible for humanity. You can follow the numbers next to the symbols to see which gate (hexagram) each planet occupies at birth. Going down the list first is the Sun, then Earth, north node, south node, the Moon, Mercury, Venus, Mars, Jupiter, Saturn, Kiron, Uranus, Neptune, and Pluto.

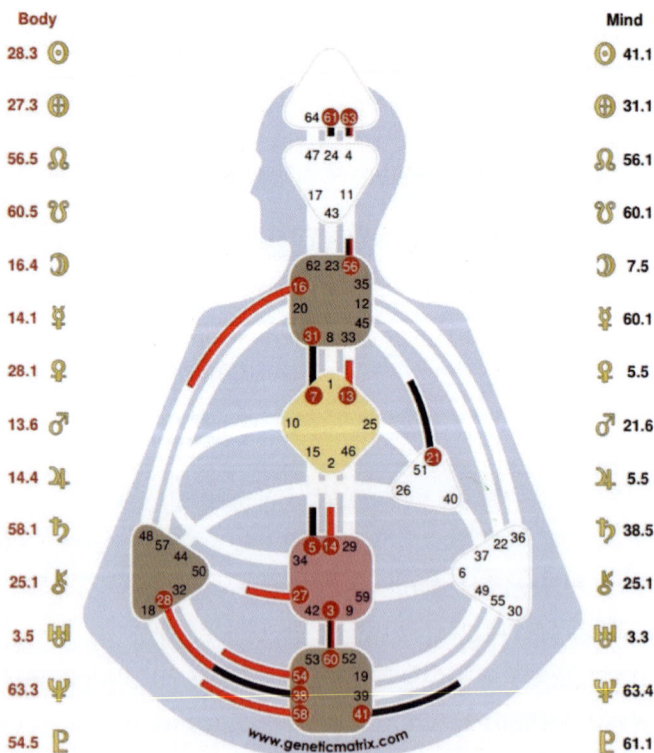

www.geneticmatrix.com

Side note: You will notice that the 41 has a second number with it: 41.1. Just to bring more complexity and richness, the Sun is not only in the 41st hexagram, but it is also in the first line (counting from the bottom up) of the hexagram. You really don't need to comprehend all this at this time, but just so you know what you're looking at, I've included the information. For this book and your work with clients at this level, it's not relevant.

THE BODYGRAPH: THE RED NUMBERS

Roughly three months before your birth (88 degrees, astrologically speaking), the neutrino stream also picked up the energies of your planets and the information from the hexagrams they were occupying and created the unconscious aspect of you. This is reflected by the red numbers.

The red in the graph is referred to as *the body, the design, the unconscious.*

In Human Design, we speak to this moment as the time when the soul landed. Because the red aspect is unconscious, when you reflect this information to your clients, they may recognize it as an aspect of themselves when it's pointed out, but because it is unconscious, they most likely don't walk around identifying with that quality. This energy is like the hand you're dealt in life. You don't have a lot of capacity to change it. The job is more to surrender and allow these energies to have their life.

In this chart, the top red number and symbol show the unconscious sun in Gate 28 (Hexagram 28). The next symbol is the unconscious earth in Gate 27 (Hexagram 27). Again, just so you get an idea of how this works, Gate 28 is the *Gate of Struggle,* so an important part of this person's life will be about struggle and learning to work with the struggles that are worthwhile to them.

PUTTING IT TOGETHER

When we transpose the black and the red numbers onto the chart, we get a person's unique chart. This is called the Triangle. This is who they are. It is the blueprint of their energy pattern that is consistent throughout their lives. To see how the numbers are transposed onto the chart above, transpose the conscious and unconscious sun.

First, look at the top black number on the right next to the sun symbol. As we said before, in this chart, that's Gate 41. To find Gate 41 on the Triangle, look at the bottom of the triangle chart and you'll see a square colored in. That square is one of the 9 centers which we call the Root Center (more on centers soon). Coming off the bottom right of that Root Center, you'll see the number 41 and a black line. That black line represents Gate 41.

To transpose the unconscious sun in this chart, look at the top left number in red next to the sun symbol which is Gate 28. Now look at the colored-in Triangle on the far left of the chart. We call this center the Spleen Center. You can see the red line in the middle channel going halfway towards the Root Center is the number 28. This represents Gate 28 (Hexagram 28).

So, for each planet, you can see which hexagram it was in either at your birth (black) or three months before your birth (red) and find the corresponding line on your chart.

There are 9 *centers*, 64 *gates*, and 32 *channels* in a chart. The gates and channels are part of a network or circuitry of flow. Let's take a look at each of these three aspects, the centers, gates, and channels, then look at what it means to be defined or open, and, finally, the flow or circuitry in the chart.

CENTERS

There are 9 *centers*. Each center is a hub, similar to chakras, holding a certain frequency or energy information system. Each center has a particular meaning and function. Whether these centers are defined (colored in) or undefined (white) tells us a lot about a person (more on this in a moment). It tells us which of the five Types a person is (see chapter 5), what their strengths and vulnerabilities are, what areas they've most likely been conditioned to believe they're someone other than who they are, and more. The centers are a powerful study in and of themselves which I hope you'll discover in the future. For now, it's enough to be familiar with the nine centers and their function:

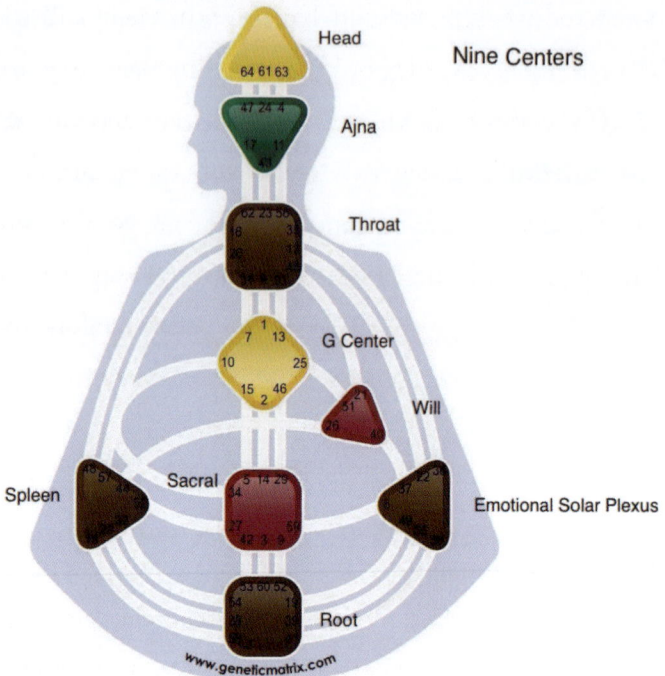

1. The Head Center: Inspiration & Ideas, a pressure center
2. The Ajna Center: Processing information
3. Throat Center: Manifestation and articulation
4. G Center/Identity Center: Self-love, direction in life, Identity
5. Will Center: Capacity to commit, Value, Material world (motor)
6. Sacral Center: Sustainable energy (motor)
7. Emotional Solar Plexus: Emotional energy (motor)
8. Spleen Center: Intuition, Fear, Time, Immune System
9. Root: Adrenalized energy (motor), a pressure center

Note: I've noted the four motors as they are instrumental in determining Type which you'll learn about in chapter 5.

THE 64 GATES

We call the hexagrams *gates*. There are 64 of them on the chart since there are 64 hexagrams. Each person will have some number of those gates defined or colored in depending on which hexagrams their planets were in at the time of their birth and three months before their birth.

If you look at the conscious sun (represented by the black line coming off the Root Center in the triangle chart that we're working with), you can see that it fills half of that channel between the Root Center at the bottom and the triangle on the right called the Emotional Solar Plexus Center, which is white in this chart.

Hanging Gates

Whenever half the channel is colored in and the other half of the channel is white, we call it a hanging gate. It doesn't matter if the gate is black or red, or both black and red; if it only fills half the channel, it is a hanging gate.

Other hanging gates in this chart are starting at the head going down: Gates 61, 63, 56, 16, 13, 21, 5, 14, 41, 54, 58.

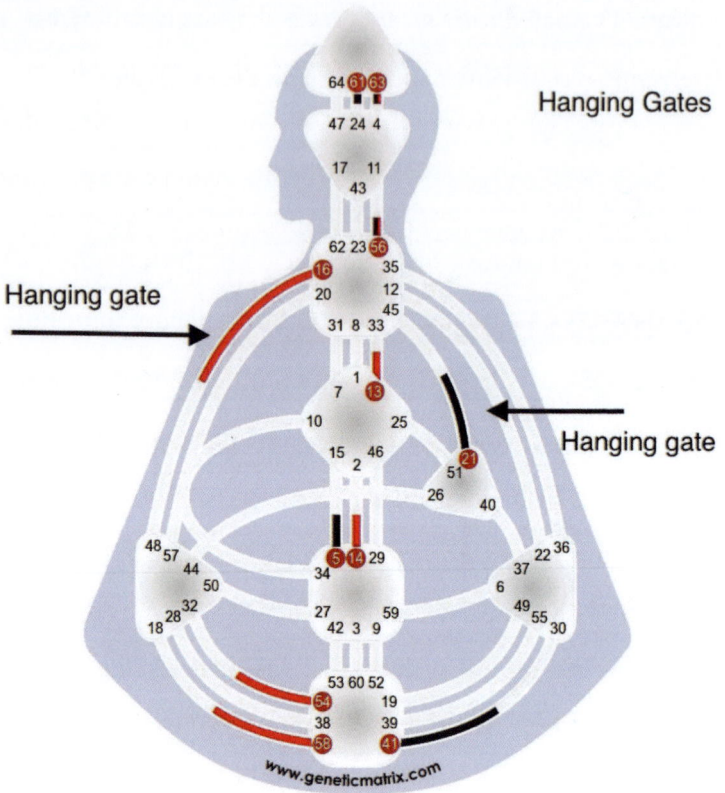

Side note: the chart is electromagnetic, which means we gravitate towards people who have the other half of that channel defined (or colored) in their chart.

32 CHANNELS

When two gates (or hexagrams) come together, they create what we call a *channel*. As there are 64 gates, when those come together, they create 32 channels. Again, it doesn't matter if the gates are black, red, or both black and red (more on that when

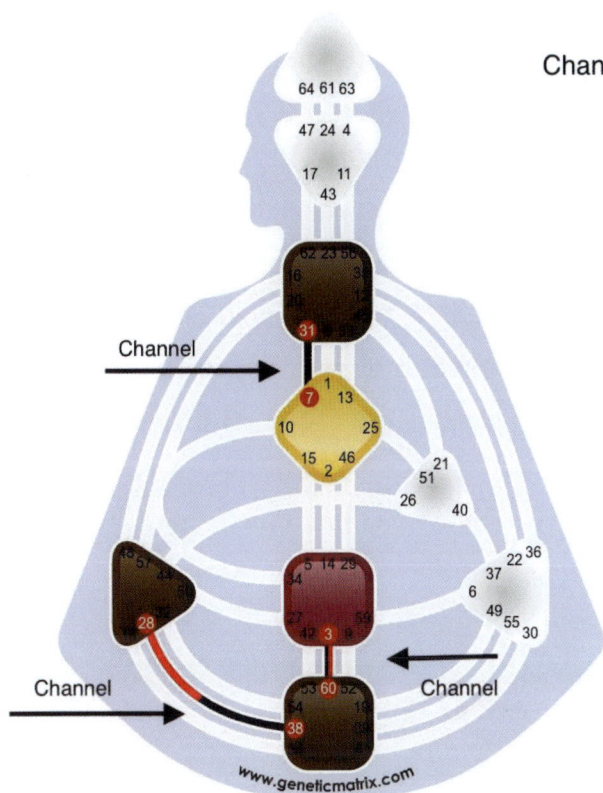

Channels

www.geneticmatrix.com

we talk about defined and undefined). What matters is that they come together, completing that circuit. In this chart, there are three defined channels:

- The Channel of Struggle combines Gate 28 from the Spleen Center and Gate 38 coming off the Root Center

- The Channel of Mutation combines Gate 3 coming down from the Sacral Center (the red square in the lower middle of the chart) and Gate 60 coming up from the Root Center

- The Channel of The Alpha combines Gate 7 coming up from the yellow diamond in the middle of the chart, the G Center, and Gate 31 coming down from the Throat Center, the brown square

When two gates form a channel, the centers on either side of the channel become defined or colored in. So, in this chart, the Throat Center, the G Center, the Sacral Center, the Root Center, and the Spleen center are all colored in.

Like the centers and gates, each of the channels carries information. For example, the Channel 28-38 is called the Channel of Struggle. People with this energy defined in their charts are designed to struggle. The important thing to note is that they enjoy struggle if it is the *right* struggle. Their job is to discern and be clear about which struggles or challenges they engage in.

DEFINED VERSUS UNDEFINED

Wherever your chart has color, we called it defined.

Wherever your chart is white, we call it open.

Definition shows up as gates, channels, and centers. Regardless of whether the gate or channel is red, black, or a combination of the two, it is defined. Likewise, wherever the chart is not colored or is white, we call that undefined. The definition or openness in a chart is key to understanding Human Design, and it has big ramifications and implications in a person's life and is often the focus of your work with them. Here you have the map to your clients' pain points, their vulnerabilities, and their strengths.

Where your clients are defined, they have consistent access to that energy. They are broadcasting that energy 24/7. For example, if your client has a defined Head Center, they are broadcasting ideas and inspiration whether they are aware of it or not. Whether they are verbalizing their ideas or not they are filling the room they occupy with thoughts. If they have the Gate 57 (coming off the Spleen Center) they have consistent access to their intuition and are broadcasting that energy, again, whether they are aware of it or not. If your clients have the Channel 34-20 the channel of power (connecting the Sacral Center and the Throat Center), the busiest channel in the whole chart, they are broadcasting activity, action, and manifestation. They are constantly in motion and sending out the message to *do*.

Where your client is undefined (i.e. where their chart is white), they are receiving the energy that's being broadcast by the people around them and by the placement of the planets in transition. Not only are they receiving the energy, but they are also amplifying it.

For instance, say your client goes to a Tony Robbins workshop. Tony Robbins has a defined Will Center. The Will Center has the energy of value and the ability to commit to something and just do it. Tony Robbins has consistent access to that Will Center energy, and so can say he's going to do something and do it. This is the core of his message. Imagine for a moment that your client has an open Will Center. At the workshop, they will be taking in and amplifying Tony Robbins' defined will energy. They will feel like they can do anything. They buy his program, all excited and ready to step into their empowered life. When they get home, they wonder, "What was I thinking?" They crash. They feel inadequate and like something is wrong with them. Nothing is wrong with them. People with defined Will Centers are designed to prove themselves. It's like flexing a muscle. People with open Will Centers are not designed to *"Just do it!"* They are not designed to prove themselves. And they can question their value because they have been conditioned to believe they get their value from what they do and that they should be more like Tony Robbins. Only a small portion of the population has a defined Will Center. The rest of us are here to be wise about value. In truth, there is nothing we can *do* to increase our value or diminish our value. Again, this is a bigger topic...

I'd like to reiterate that just like you can't change your birth time, your bodygraph does not change throughout your lifetime. Where you are defined, you will always be defined. Where you are open you will always be open. Think of it as your body: you can change your hair color, lose or gain weight, or do surgery on your body, but you can't change bodies with someone else. You have your body throughout your lifetime. Your bodygraph is like the blueprint of your energetic body mechanics.

Each place you are defined in your chart has a high expression and a low expression. How you are in relation to your definition can and does change your experience of life. Take Gate 47 for instance. This is the Mindset gate. It is right brain circuitry, trying to make sense of right-brain information (non-linear, non-logical) downloads. With Gate 47, you need to maintain a good mindset. When you do, you are available for the insights, miracles, and epiphanies that come your way. If you have a negative mindset, on the other hand, you will miss the gifts that show up to bring openings in your world and to the people around you. We could say that Human Design is a right-brain download. If Ra had been in a foul mood, pessimistic, and shut down to the light in his room, I might not be writing about this today.

Like the defined centers, the open centers do not inherently change over your lifetime. They will always remain open. However, where your clients are open they are designed to experience the full range of that energy. While it's true they won't have consistent access to the particular energy, they are here to be wise about it and designed to be fluid in those areas. Where your clients are open, they're taking on the energies of those around them. Especially as children, it is where your clients tend to be conditioned to believe they are someone they are not. In other words, they get caught in the web of living someone else's puzzle piece. The openness in your client's chart is often where their pain points show up. It's where the ego, not having something solid to hold on to, gets quite confused about who it is and grabs onto an identity regardless of what it is or whose it is.

CIRCUITRY

The channels create different kinds of circuits on the body-graph, and the circuitry speaks to the evolutionary process. This is a big topic that requires further study when you are ready. But it's important to at least introduce you to this aspect as it will come up when we look at Emotional Authority in chapter 12. The channels form circuitry systems. There are fundamentally three kinds of circuits: individual, tribal, and collective. These reflect the evolutionary process.

Individual

To evolve, we need to bring something new into the picture, something that didn't exist before. An individual energy is required. If someone has prominent individual energy in their gates or channels, part of their path is to bring something new to the planet. Someone with access to Individual Circuitry envisioned and introduced the first electric car in the 1830s, but it couldn't compete with the popular and cheaper combustion engine. What the individual brings is tested by the tribe, the next level of circuitry, which determines whether the new idea survives and is integrated at a larger level or falls away.

Individual Circuitry

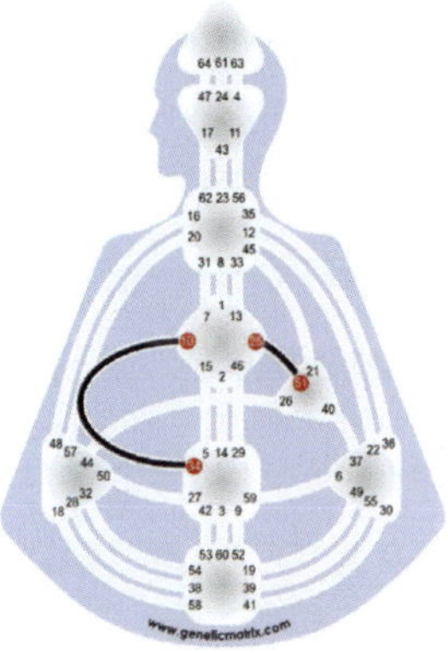

Centering Circuit

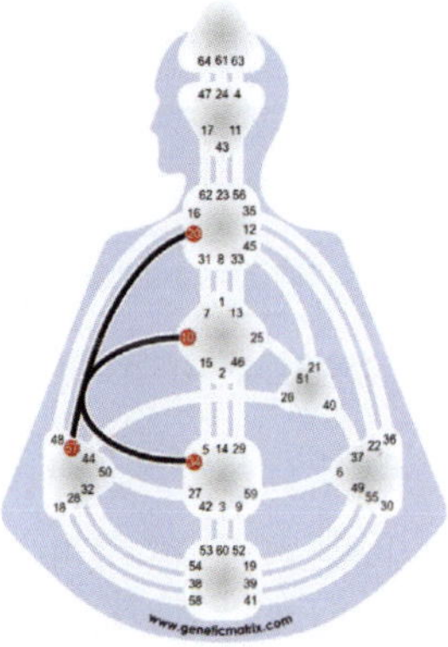

Integration Circuit

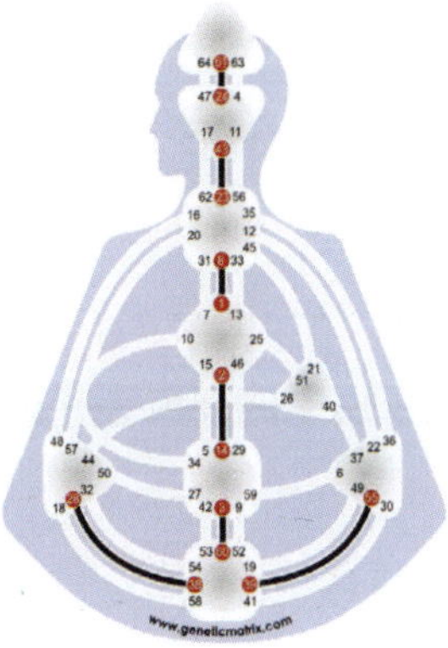

Knowing Circuit

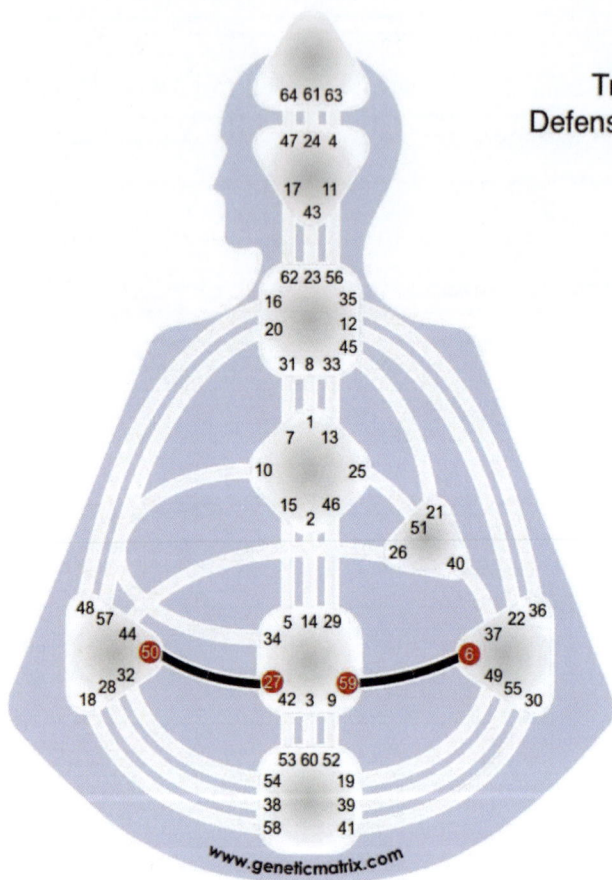

Tribal
Defense Circuit

www.geneticmatrix.com

Tribal

The second type of circuitry is called Tribal. It is the energy engaged with the survival of the tribe: sex, war, food, education, values, negotiations. It is a passionate and fiery energy. What an individual brings to the tribe is either accepted or rejected.

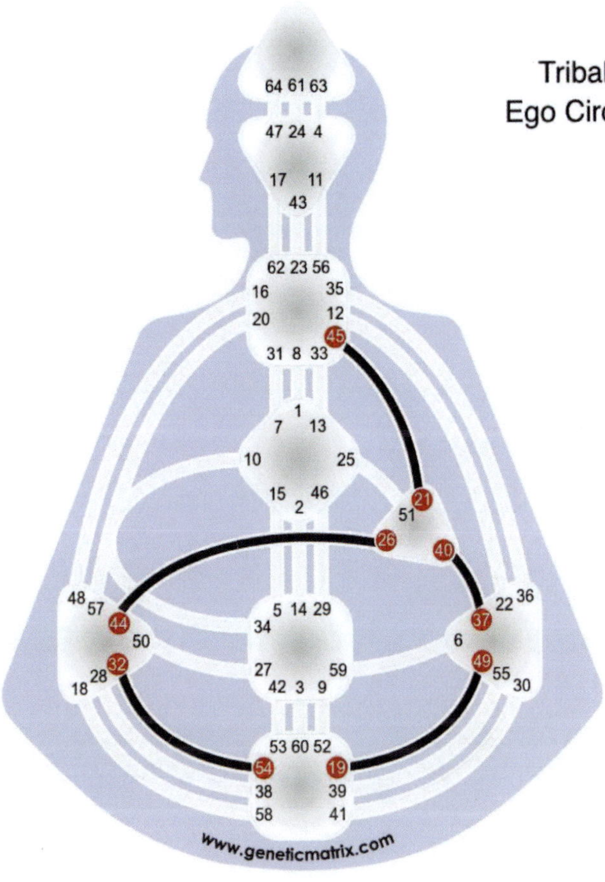

Tribal
Ego Circuit

www.geneticmatrix.com

After being initially rejected, electric cars weren't integrated into the tribe until the need to protect our resources for the health and future of the planet became pressing and this technology was deemed vital to our survival.

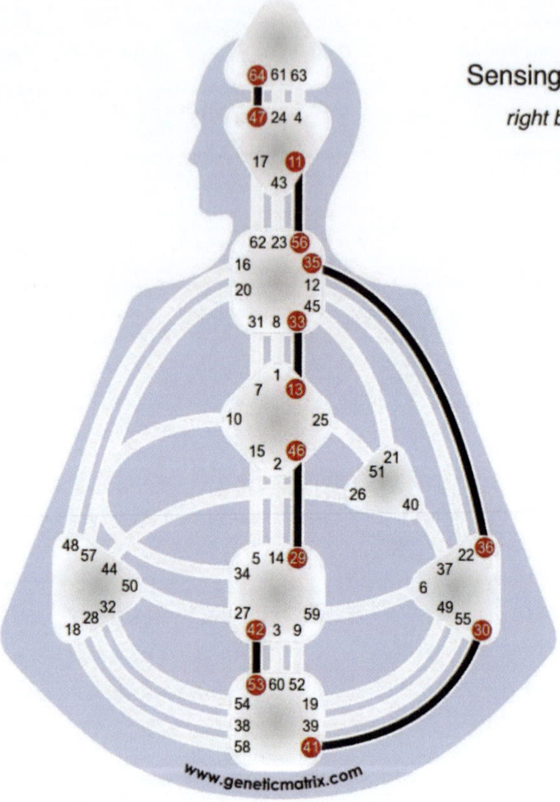

Sensing Circuit

right brain

www.geneticmatrix.com

Collective

Once the new idea or invention is accepted by the tribe, we could say it's brought to the next circuitry – the collective circuitry – to be tested and, again, either accepted or rejected. The collective circuitry is about structures: government, school systems, laws, rules, and regulations. It is concerned with sharing information. In the example of the electric car, the government

54

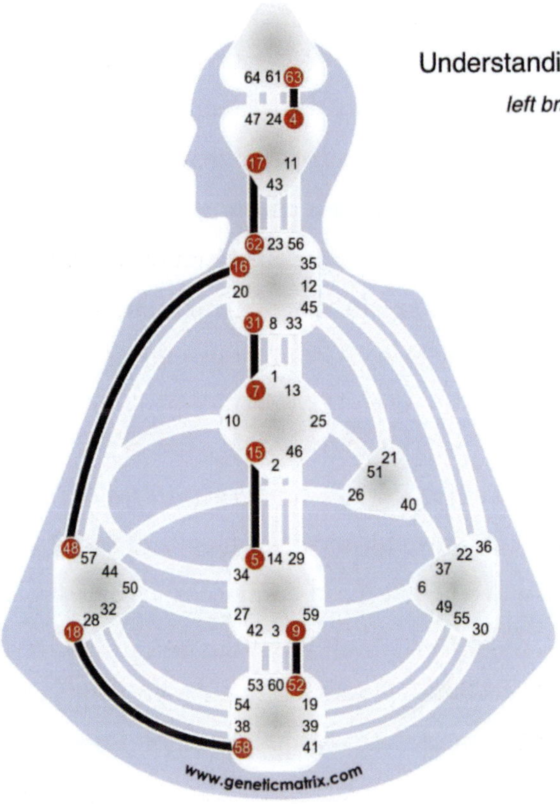

Understanding Circuit

left brain

www.geneticmatrix.com

determines that the air quality is affected by dirty emissions and requires newer technology in cars. If you have an electric car, you are given certain rebates from the government to subsidize the more expensive new technology and encourage people to buy electric. At some point, we can imagine it could be illegal to drive anything but electric cars.

All of this is to say that the amount of individual, tribal, or collective circuitry a person has in their chart will influence how they operate in the world. A person with strong individual circuitry could be challenged by someone with strong tribal circuitry. And someone who has both strong individual circuitry and strong tribal circuitry within them could understandably have some internal conflicts: do they follow their creative individual inclination or do they follow their tribal instinct to belong and fit in?

THE NEXT PIECE: TYPE AND STRATEGY

Now that you have the basic understanding of elements in the chart, you are ready to put them together to understand and make sense of the five Types with their accompanying strategy, as well as the four Authorities. In the next chapter, I'll explain the mechanics of how the Types are determined, and, in chapter 12, we'll look specifically at Authority.

CHAPTER 5

UNDERSTANDING THE FIVE BASIC TYPES AND STRATEGY

I f you think of Human Design as a giant puzzle with each piece representing a human being, there are roughly 8 billion puzzle pieces. Each piece is unique, yet some have similar qualities. There are five fundamental puzzle pieces. So, there are five types of people: Generators, Manifesting Generators, Manifestors, Projectors, and Reflectors. Each Type has an operating system, a Strategy to best navigate in the world. Each Type is here to bring something to humanity in a particular way and will have challenges that accompany it.

In the same way that no one puzzle piece is more important than another in the big picture, no person's unique design or Type is more important than any other. We need all the pieces to complete the puzzle. We need blue sky pieces. We need green grass pieces.

That is not to say that some pieces, some Types, aren't more idealized in our culture and that some pieces and Types don't have more challenges than others. Those challenges don't diminish one's value. The greatest challenges come not from our Type but from not knowing, not being aligned with, or fighting against our Type. Not living in alignment with our Type and Strategy creates havoc in our lives. It's like trying to force a puzzle piece into the wrong place in the puzzle. It just doesn't work. On the other hand, when we live according to our Type, Strategy, and Authority, we're in harmony with ourselves, we align with the universe, and we enter the flow. We're rowing down the stream rather than fighting the current. As we surrender to who we are, we're able to enter the mystery of life in a co-creative empowered way. We stop trying to do something other than our design. Humanity is an interconnected web, interdependent on each of us living our piece. As we live our piece, we support the evolution of humanity. That is the core purpose of Human Design. It was downloaded to support our evolution on the planet.

The Types are determined by what is defined and what is open in the chart. Or another way to think of it is how the energy flows in a chart. Each Type has a particular function and Strategy. Here we'll lay out the basic mechanics of the Types, and in later chapters, we'll focus on each Type and how to work with clients who have that Type.

THE FIVE TYPES

The Generator

Whenever the Sacral Center is defined, the person's Type is automatically a Generator or Manifesting Generator. Manifesting Generators are first and foremost Generators, so while we classify them separately, it's important to know that anything true for a Generator is also fundamentally the case for a Manifesting Generator. Therefore, if you see that red square on the chart you know you're working with Generator energy.

Roughly seventy percent of the population have the Sacral Center defined. So, chances are likely that most of your clients will be Generators or Manifesting Generators. The Sacral Center is one of what we call the four motors in the chart (see chart #12). The Sacral motor is the biggest motor in the chart and functions like, well, a generator motor, that is either turned on or off. When the Sacral motor is turned on, the person has sustainable vital life force energy available to them. When it's turned off … not so much. This binary on/off motor is designed to respond to the world around it by either resonating and switching on, or not resonating and switching off. The Sacral Center motor often makes a humming sound like a motor an *uh-huh*, when it resonates, or an *uh-uh* when it doesn't. This will be important information that will inform your work with your Generator and Manifesting Generator clients.

The folks who have this Sacral Center motor are designed to work. Their life purpose is to discover the right livelihood and master their work. This is a dharmic activity and brings great pleasure. If you think of a beehive or an ant colony, the Generators are the worker bees and ants responsible for creating the hives or colonies. They go to all lengths to carry out their sacred task, building the structures that allow life to flourish.

The Sacral Center motors have sustainable energy, as long as they are following their Sacral *yeses* and *nos*. When the Generator types are not taught or ignore their Sacral motor, overriding the information to go forward or not, they risk burnout, dissatisfaction, and frustration. It's been said that the world is so messed up right now because so many Generators and Manifesting Generators are doing work they have a *no* for.

The Generator's Sacral Center motor acts like a battery pack that is designed to be used all day long. It is optimal for Generators to use their motor during the day, fall asleep exhausted at night, and wake up with their battery pack recharged ready to go the next morning. You'll see when I talk about working with your Generator clients that I refer to them as working dogs. If you've ever had a working dog, you know how important it is to give them a job and exercise them to point of exhaustion!

The Sacral Center motor of the Generators and Manifesting Generators is an inner GPS, available at all times to guide them in all areas of life. Once you understand the power of this guidance system, you can appreciate the value of these Sacral

Center motor types. You can also imagine the power of learning to listen and trust that motor.

The Generator Strategy: Wait to Respond

Because Generators are guided by this motor and its response to outside stimuli, the best strategy for them to navigate their lives is *to wait to respond.* In other words, Generators are not designed to initiate action; they are meant to be in relationship to life, waiting for their motor to be turned on before they take action. Waiting and honoring our inner guidance is not a cultural value and can be difficult to reorient.

The Emotional Theme
for the Generator: Frustration

In the journey of mastering work, Generators hit plateaus. When this happens, they can become frustrated and question what they're doing. Do they still have a *yes?* Or is it time to quit this project and shift to another? Navigating this terrain is an important part of the Generator path. If the Generator has a habit of quitting when things get hard then you know something is off. They must learn to tolerate the plateaus and discern when it is not a good direction and when they've hit the learning bump, perhaps needing to re-tweak what they're doing rather than abandon the task or the relationship.

These are the channels that create a Generator chart.

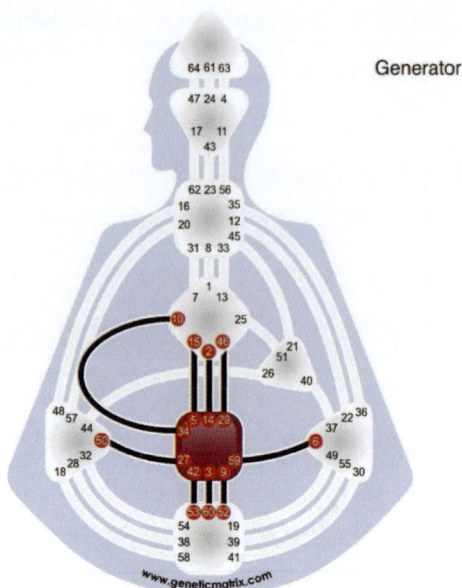

Generator

The Manifesting Generator

As you saw above, when the chart shows a defined (red) Sacral Center it is the chart of a Generator. Manifesting Generators are fundamentally Generators. They have all the attributes we listed above that come with the Generator motor, namely they have sustainable energy and are here to master work. That motor turns on and off, so Manifesting Generators must wait to respond before acting.

So what makes them a Manifesting Generator? It's adding a motor to the Throat Center. Let me take a moment to explain what a motor to Throat Center looks like mechanically and what the ramifications are when someone has a motor to the Throat Center.

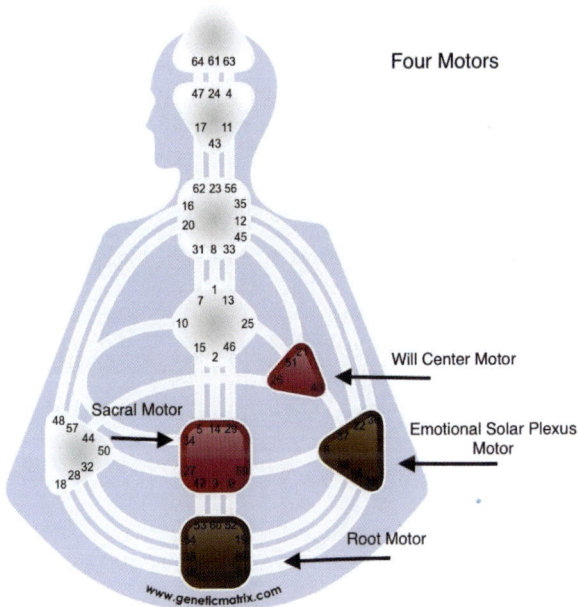

Four Motors

64 61 63

47 24 4

17 11
43

62 23 56
16   35
20   12
           45
31 8 33

1
7 13
10   25
15 46
2

Will Center Motor

Sacral Motor

48
57
44
50
32
28
18

Emotional Solar Plexus
Motor

Root Motor

www.geneticmatrix.com

To begin, we've established that the Sacral Center was one of four motors. The other motors are:

- The Will Center
- The Emotional Solar Plexus Center
- The Root Center

If any of these motors have a channel going to the throat, it is called a motor to the throat. The next chart shows two ways a motor can get to the throat: one is direct, the Channel 34-20, and the other meanders through the chart connecting the Channel 3-60 from the Sacral Center (motor) to the Root Center (motor), then the 28-38 from the Root Center to the Spleen Center (non-motor), and finally, the Channel 48-16 up to the Throat Center.

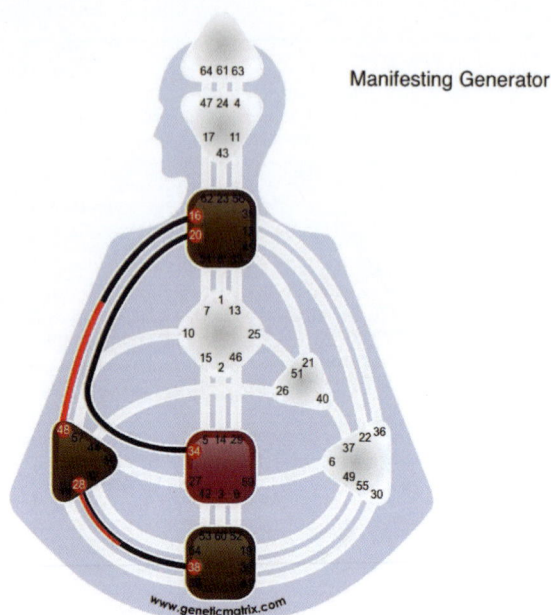

Manifesting Generator

www.geneticmatrix.com

All Manifestors have a motor to the throat. That is the definition of a Manifestor. We'll get to pure Manifestors next, but for now, having a motor to the throat (whether you are a Manifesting Generator or a Manifestor) means you can manifest. Remember the Bible quote "In the beginning was the word..."? When energy from one of the motors gets to the throat, then what we say has power and force. It enables us to create. It impacts others. It can be heard. Whole worlds are created when there is a motor to the throat. We say that if Human Design were a game, the way to win it is to get a motor to the throat. For those of us who do not have a motor to the throat, we are driven to connect with people who have one or electromagnetically give us one. Manifesting Generators empower people just by their presence.

The Manifesting Generator not only has sustainable energy, but it also has consistent access to the energy of impacting and creating. But this power is only available in response to the Sacral Center. Manifesting Generators are uniquely designed to move quickly and to multitask. They are highly capable and often prefer to handle things themselves rather than explain to someone else what to do.

The Manifesting Generator Strategy: To Wait to Respond, Inform, Then Act

Because Manifesting Generators have the Sacral Center, they are designed to live in response. Thus, they must wait for the Sacral Center to be turned on before engaging. It is not enough for a Manifesting Generator to have the thought "I need a vacation," then book a vacation. They need something from the outside world to flip that switch. Say their best friend says, "You look like you could use a vacation." The Sacral turns on, they have a *yes* response. But they can't just go book the vacation; they need to inform their boss, partner, or whomever it will impact. There's a tendency to want to act on their own, but when they inform, they have a better possible outcome. That Manifestor part can feel dominant to others – and we resist that!

The Emotional Theme for Manifesting Generator: Frustration and Anger

Like the Generator, when the Manifesting Generator's momentum is disturbed or plateaus, the Generator part gets frustrated. The Manifestor part gets angry. This can be a knee-jerk reaction, and while not condoning it, understanding that this is the design can bring some space and compassion to a pattern that will need to be worked with.

The Manifestor

If the chart has an open (white) Sacral Center and one of the other three motors going to the throat you've got the chart of a Manifestor. Only 8 percent of the population are Manifestors. In this chart, you can see all the ways the Will Center motor, the Root Center motor, and the Emotional Solar Plexus Center motor can get to the throat.

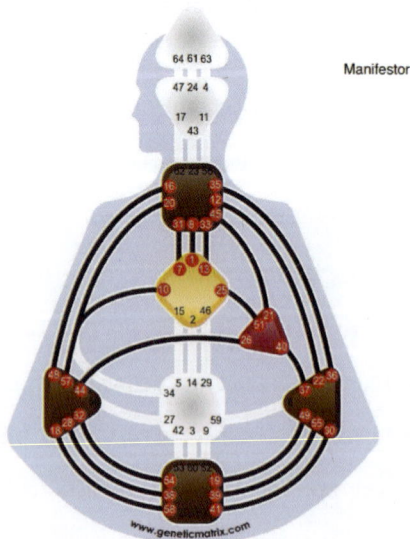

Manifestor

www.geneticmatrix.com

Unlike Manifesting Generators and Generators, the Manifestor's Sacral Center is white or open. This means they do not have that Sacral Center motor. They do not have sustainable energy. They do not have that inner GPS. That open Sacral Center takes in and amplifies all the Generator energy around them, so they can do more than any Generator or Manifesting Generator – for a period of time. But they cannot sustain the energy, and they burn out if they try to act like Generators. Manifestors need more rest than Generators and need to be by themselves away from the Generator energy to dissipate the motor rev. With the open Sacral Center, Manifestors are vulnerable to not knowing when enough is enough and can overdo.

Manifestors (and anyone with an open Sacral Center) are not designed to work like Generators. That is not their dharma. Manifestors are here to impact people, situations, and projects. They are here to get things moving. They are designed to initiate a process, then step out and let the Generators do the footwork. Because Manifestors don't have that Sacral motor, they don't have to wait to respond in the same way someone with a defined Sacral Center does. On the other hand, without the clear Sacral guidance system, Manifestors often don't know what's going to work until they try it. We call it the spaghetti-on-the-wall approach. Manifestors don't know if the spaghetti's done until they throw it on the wall and see if it sticks. Some of my Manifestor colleagues speak about developing an inner-body-based knowing that helps guide them, but this is one of the Manifestor challenges.

Manifestors are powerful forces with a closed and repelling aura. They're often referred to as the generals of humanity and have typically been the leaders of our culture. Having a motor to the throat means they don't depend on others to take action, and as a result, they can be loners. They are designed to act independently. When a Manifestor walks into a room, you feel their potency. Because Manifestors have their sense of authority and don't tolerate being dominated, they can be difficult to parent. Often, they can be like stallions that get broken into submission, losing touch with their power and potency, silencing their creative impactful voices.

Manifestors have a non-verbal process that requires time. They need to be allowed to be in their flow in their creative process. They don't do well when people try to help them or interrupt their flow. It's important to give Manifestors the time to complete their thoughts before jumping in.

The Manifestor Strategy: To Inform

Because Manifestors are so powerful and impactful, they can be intimidating or challenging to others. Manifestors are designed to do what they want to do when they want to do it. This is not always welcomed in our culture! When Manifestors inform people of what they're going to do, they stand a better chance of diminishing resistance. It's not an act of asking for permission; it's truly informing.

The Emotional Theme for the Manifestor: Anger

When Manifestors are interrupted in their process or when things don't go the way the Manifestor wants, they get angry. This can be tough both for the Manifestor and for the people around them and is something that will need to be worked with without shutting down their creative power.

The Projector

If the chart has a white or open Sacral and *no motor* to the Throat Center, you're working with a Projector. Twenty-one percent of the population are Projectors. They are often referred to as the wise guides of humanity. Projectors are here to direct and guide people and energy. They have a focused aura and are tuned in to the people around them. Their particular puzzle piece is often undervalued and misunderstood in our culture. We are at a crossroads in our evolution, shifting from Manifestor leadership to Projector leadership, but until that shift is established, Projectors can have a tough go. Like Manifestors, Projectors have the open Sacral Center, so they don't have consistent access to sustainable energy, they don't have the inner GPS motor, they're not designed to work like Generators, and they don't know when enough is enough so they often overdo and exhaust themselves. They also need to get out of the Generator field to discharge all the energy they've picked up during the day. They need more rest than Generator types and should go to bed before they're tired. Believing they should act like Generators, they often burn out by the time they're in their thirties.

The Projector Strategy: Wait for an Invitation; Wait to Be Acknowledged

Without a motor to the throat that the Manifestors have, Projectors don't have consistent access to taking action or initiating and are only empowered to do so once they are invited or acknowledged. This is tricky, and there is often a sense of not being seen or a feeling of impotency with Projectors which they sometimes counteract by exaggerating their visibility. When this doesn't work, they can become bitter. On the other hand, an empowered Projector is inspiring and moves the Generator energy into action. We can look to famous Projectors who inspired the nation – Obama and JFK as examples.

As Projectors learn to be skillful with their puzzle piece, not throwing their pearls before swine but instead waiting for the right moment to share their wisdom, they take their rightful empowered place.

The Emotional Theme for the Projector:
Bitterness

Because the Projector isn't designed to assert themselves on their own behalf and because our culture is so Manifestor- and Generator-oriented, Projectors can easily feel unseen, unacknowledged, and undervalued. Knowing they have something important to give but not having an arena where their offering is being received can leave the Projector feeling disempowered and bitter.

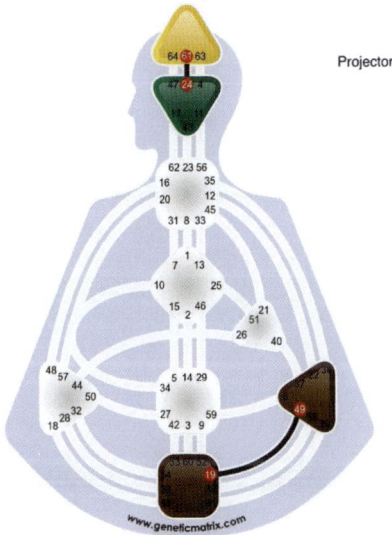

Projector

www.geneticmatrix.com

The Reflector

If there are no channels and no centers defined (in other words, all the centers are white), you've got the chart of a Reflector. This is the rarest of all the Types, as only 1 percent of the population are Reflectors. This Type is taking in and amplifying all the energies around them. The most unusual, Reflectors are also the most challenging for the rest of the Types to understand. In a way, there is very little consistent substance to Reflectors who are profoundly fluid, shifting identities and their sense of self almost moment to moment with each new person, place, or planetary shift they encounter. Designed to reflect the health and well-being (or lack of health and well-being) of the energy around them, Reflectors are like the canary in the coal mine. They play a particular role in the puzzle, and as we learn to recognize and support their piece we gain access to important information about ourselves and our communities.

Like the other open Sacral Types, Reflectors take in the Sacral energy around them, need to learn when enough is enough, and are vulnerable to burnout. They need more rest than the Generator Types and they need to get out of the Generator field to unwind and restore their energy.

The Reflector Strategy: Wait Before Making Decisions (Recommended Twenty-Nine Days)

Because the Reflector is so fluid, taking in the thoughts, energies, feelings, identities, and pressures of everyone around them, they need time to get clear on what they think or feel after processing all that energy. The standard thought is that Reflectors must wait one lunar cycle, or twenty-nine days, although some of the Reflectors I know have called this specific time frame into question.

The Emotional Theme for Reflectors: Disappointment

Reflectors are so open and naturally take people in so deeply, seeing what's possible for them, that when people fall short, the Reflector can be left disappointed sometimes in a devastated or heartbreaking way.

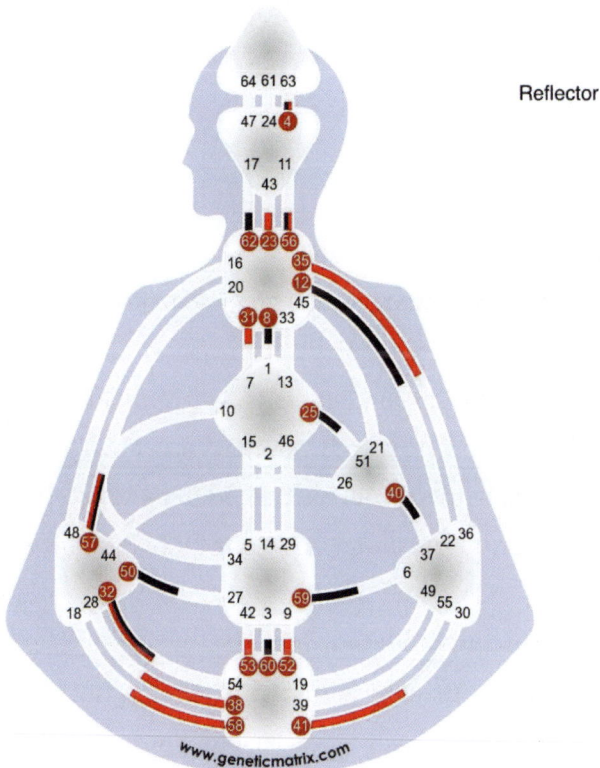

Reflector

www.geneticmatrix.com

QUICK REVIEW TYPES AND STRATEGIES

- Generators
  - Have defined Sacral Centers and no motor to the throat
  - Their Strategy is to respond
- Manifesting Generators
  - Have a defined Sacral Center and a motor to the throat
  - Their Strategy is to respond and inform
- Manifestors
  - Have an open Sacral Center and a motor to the throat
  - Their Strategy is to inform
- Projectors
  - Have an open Sacral Center and no motor to the throat
  - Their Strategy is to wait for the invitation
- Reflectors
  - Have no centers defined
  - Their Strategy is to wait twenty-nine days before acting or making decisions

As we shift to Section 3, we begin the process of putting this foundational information to use with your clients. In the next chapter, you'll learn how to run a chart, and then in chapters 7 through 11, you'll learn how to take the information from this chapter and put it into action with your clients. You'll be shown the implications of each of these Types, how they best navigate the world, how to work with their Strategy, what some of their gifts and challenges are, and how to best approach each of these Types when they are your clients.

Section 3

Working with Clients – Human Design in Action

CHAPTER 6

GETTING STARTED

You've made it through the learning curve of the mechanics of the Human Design chart in chapters 4 and 5, or perhaps you're diving in to look at charts right away. In any event, there are a few things you will want to consider as you begin to put Human Design into action.

GETTING THE TYPE: RUNNING THE CHART

To get your client's Type, you will need to have their accurate birth information to run their chart. That means, their birth time, place, and date. You can run charts on many sites, but I recommend freehumandesignchart.com, as it is highly accurate. You simply input the birth information and a chart will be available immediately. If you want to keep track of your charts and possibly use a professional service, I recommend GeneticMatrix.com.

If you cannot get an accurate birth time, you are left with three options:

1. Nix using this system with that person/client

2. Hire someone to help you discern the time

3. Spend a little time yourself inputting various times during the day to see how much the chart changes

Sometimes it doesn't change much at all. At this entry point, I would just check to see if the Type, Authority, or Profile change. (The Profile will be noted on the chart.) If the chart does change, you're going to want to consult with someone about the questions you would ask to get the right time. It's usually not hard to determine once you know what to look for and what questions to ask. If it's still unclear, you can have an astrologer do a time rectification chart where they look at the major events in your client's life and can pinpoint their birth time. It's much easier if the time is known from a reliable source.

START WITH YOURSELF

Begin by running your chart and looking at your Type.

Once you have your Type, you can skip to that particular chapter and read about yourself. Chapters 7 through 11 look at the 5 different Types and their Strategies. If you are looking at the chart of a Manifesting Generator, first read the Generator section, as that applies to the Manifesting Generator as well.

This is where the fun begins. What does your chart say about you? Does it make sense? Does it resonate? Are you surprised by what it shows? You might be sparked to have a personal reading by a Human Design Specialist: https://www.quantum-alignmentsystem.com/human-design/readings.

Do not skip this step! Knowing your chart is the basis of working with your client. For example, if you know you are a Manifestor, this knowledge will impact how you work with clients. You have capacities most of your clients will not have. You can initiate action. If you are thinking that other people should be able to do what you do and how you do it, you are not taking into account your differences. You must also learn to inform your clients of what you're going to do (suggest, require, etc.) or risk them feeling dominated or disempowered. Understanding your chart will ground you in the transformational process and empower your work.

Next, run the charts of your family members, friends, and co-workers you know well. This is a way to get a sense of the system from an engaging and compelling place. As you familiarize yourself with the various types, you'll begin to recognize the different characteristics and start to develop confidence. As you begin to understand their charts, you may be surprised by the understanding that begins to come through. For example, when I ran my mom's chart, I discovered she was a Manifestor. That gave me a new perspective on her, and why her parenting style was so challenging for me. Finally, after you've played with your own, your family's, friends', and coworkers' charts, you can begin running your clients' charts.

WHEN THE CHART IS NOT A FIT

If someone does not seem like or identify with the Type on their chart, there are two possibilities: one, you've got the wrong birth time, or two, and the more likely case, they are living out of conditioning – who they think they should be – rather than who they truly are. For example, Manifestors are powerhouses. They are here to impact people. This Type can be challenging for parents who often try to break the spirit of these children. You will find clients who are surprised that they are Manifestors, as that truth has been, we could say, beaten out of them. The work is to support them to reclaim their puzzle piece. You may recognize them as a Manifestor by their rebuffing aura or other obvious indicators that fit the type. They just may not recognize their power, potency, or the impact they have on others. I had a Manifestor client who was going through life like she was riding a bicycle when she had the chart of someone riding a Harley. The moment she walked into the room, I knew I was with big energy. She just didn't initially recognize herself like that.

HUMAN DESIGN AND SUFFERING

Our clients come to us because they're struggling with a problem or problems. They're suffering. They don't like something in their lives. From the Buddhist view, it's fundamentally an attachment or aversion issue. People either want something they don't have or are trying to get away from something they do have. This could be themselves, their feelings, their habits, their relationships, their work, their finances, their lifestyle — whatever. The issue our clients bring is the presenting problem: the starting place. As practitioners, we know that solving the "issue" is the desired byproduct, but the real goal is to get to the root of the problem and resolve that.

I have a brother-in-law who was overweight since childhood. He was bullied and suffered horribly as a result. His entire life, he desperately wanted to be thin. As an adult and a successful chiropractor, this weight issue continued to haunt him. He chose to have his stomach stapled. He lost the weight, looked great, and was very happy with the results. He had "solved" the presenting problem. What he didn't take into account was the underlying problem that caused the weight issue in the first place. Like many people who have that surgery, he transferred his habit of eating to self-soothe and manage a tough childhood into a habit of drinking. He died of alcoholism in his fifties. After his death, I read an article that spoke to this problem of people having the surgery and then taking on often worse coping mechanisms that led to debilitating lifestyles or death.

NOT A QUICK FIX

Learning Human Design is not going to be like that staple surgery. It's not going to solve your clients' presenting problems. It's not a quick fix or a band-aid. What it will do is help you understand your client better right out of the gate. With new clients, you'll have access to a whole database of information to support your work with them. It also gives you a way to empower your clients so they can get some distance from their long-held beliefs about themselves. When your clients recognize themselves, when they're seen, something shifts. It's like that story of the snake and the rope. Once they see it's a rope, they can't scare themselves by thinking they're in danger. Once they know their Type, it's no longer an issue of being a failure because their father told them they were worthless. That happened, yes, and needs to be seen and understood for its part. But that's not the underlying problem getting in the way of them doing what they came to do. The question is: are they aligned with the truth of who they are so they can show up fully. If they're good with themselves, the world quickly becomes a playground or a canvas – full of possibility.

In the cosmology of Human Design, we are not designed to suffer. There is no suffering in the chart. There is struggle, there is shock, there is control, there are extremes, there are challenges, but there is not a marker for suffering. Your clients suffer when they think they should be a different puzzle piece. They suffer when they try to be someone they are not. They suffer when they don't live their design. And, they can suffer when they live at the low end of their design.

Just as it wouldn't make sense to think that a puzzle piece that was depicting blue sky should be showing grass, it would not make sense for a Projector to think they should act and behave like a Generator. But with 70 percent of the population being Generators and Manifesting Generators, we *do* assume that everyone should operate with inexhaustible energy and make their life's purpose their work. This is the mess we find ourselves in when we ascribe to the cultural norm rather than acknowledging, honoring, and celebrating differences.

As you turn to look at your clients through the lens of Type, keep in mind that people may not be happy with their Type at first. The inclination to compare and contrast is so embedded in our psyches. As you approach each client's Type with the curiosity, respect, and compassion they deserve, your clients will have a better chance at exploring and embracing their innate operating system revealed through Human Design.

CHAPTER 7

UNDERSTANDING YOUR GENERATOR CLIENT

Generators are like working dogs; they're full of energy, vitality, and purpose. They have a job to do and are here to do it. The more energy they expend doing what they are called to do, the more content they are. Like dogs, they are responding to everything around them. If they smell something, they want to follow it. You can pull on their leash, but if they don't want to go, they will stop. Generators have to train themselves to focus and harness their energy. Again, like dogs, Generators are deeply relational. Your Generator clients are here to find their right work and master it. The majority of your clients will be Generators or Manifesting Generators. Most of what I say in this chapter about Generators will also apply to Manifesting Generators, who are first and foremost Generators because they have a defined Sacral Center (see chapter 5). These two Types comprise 70 percent of the population. Generators are the workforce of humanity. Some people are initially disappointed when they find out they are Generators. You'll hear people say, "I'm *just* a Generator." They can feel like they are not special, or as if they are chained to work and slaves to *doing*. They mistakenly believe Generators are not as powerful as some of the other Types. Just for clarification, Oprah Winfrey, one of the most powerful women alive today, is "just" a Generator. Oh, and then there's the Generator Dalai Lama.

This is a gentle reminder that each person is unique and is here to bring something for the evolution of humanity. A puzzle piece that shows grass is no less important than one that shows a flower. All the pieces are equally needed to complete the picture. Not only that, but the bodygraph design is not an egoic identity. Rather, it is the structure through which you can live your true expression of yourself. When you consider the power of limits, your design shapes how energy flows most naturally in and through you. When you are no longer resisting that structure, you are freed to live in a deeply empowering way.

RECOGNIZE AND SUPPORT THE GENERATOR'S GIFTS

The Generator is laden with powerful gifts:

1. Sustainable energy
2. Inner GPS
3. Responsive nature
4. Proclivity to find and master their life's work
5. Relational capacity

The Gift of Sustainable Energy

When a Generator's motors are turned on, their capacity to generate can be mind-boggling. They have a tremendous amount of life force energy available to them. Going back to the analogy of working dogs, Generators get more energy from working than from resting. They are fulfilled by their work and through their work. Like those dogs, Generators need an activity that exhausts them. When I first came to live on Maui, I went into a Projector-like vacation mode. While it was good for a time, I discovered I was missing the stimulation that my Generator-self needed. It was depleting me to not be engaged and not to have things to respond to. Generators are designed to work all day long, fall asleep exhausted at night, and wake up the next morning battery recharged, ready to go. As a Generator, I can imagine working as long as I'm alive. It's rejuvenating and the right action for a Generator to use the Sacral Center motor in alignment with what turns them on.

The Gift of the Inner GPS

Next to their endless access to sustainable energy, perhaps the greatest advantage Generators have over other types is their inner GPS. Their Sacral Center motor enables them to respond to life with a clear uh-huh (*yes*) or uh-uh (*no*). This is a huge asset. I had a client come to Maui for an intensive recently. She was from Brazil, and her phone didn't pick up a signal here. She had bought the GPS for the rental car but lost the cord to plug it in; she had to navigate with maps and by the directions we gave her. I live in rural Maui and getting to my home is tricky. She got lost on more than one occasion. One night, I ended up on Piiholo Road in the rain waiting for her car to drive by so I could flash my lights and show her the way through the forest. This is what people without a defined Sacral Center, or people not tuned into their Sacral Center, are up against most of the time – navigating without a clear inner GPS.

The Gift of a Responsive Nature

Generators are in a dance with the universe. They don't have to figure anything out. The universe shows up; the Generator responds with their Sacral Center motor and is guided. It's like the universe is the lead dancer and all the Generator has to do is follow its cues. The best strategy for the Generator is to wait until something comes into their field and then respond. This takes a certain level of trust and openness to their environment and their surroundings.

Before coming to Maui, my wife and I moved from the Bay Area to Iowa. The house on the lake that we thought we were buying fell through, and we found ourselves living at my sister's while we looked for a rental. Everywhere we looked, my Sacral Center had a blaring *no.* Our realtor just happened to drive through a part of town that didn't have rentals but was beautiful. I immediately said, "I could live here." No sooner had I said that than a friend of my sister's (who was taking a walk in the neighborhood) waved at us. My sister told her we were looking for a place to rent and the woman said a friend of hers might be renting a house in this neighborhood. Within an hour, we were standing in a 5,000 square foot *Gone With the Wind*-style mansion with a spiral staircase, 1,000 square foot great room with floor-to-ceiling windows, expansive rolling green grass, and a view of the lake. All of that came at a ridiculously affordable price. My Sacral Center was a full-on *yes*. We had found our home.

The Gift of the Proclivity to Finding and Mastering Their Life's Work

Generators are driven to find fulfilling work. There's a sense of ease that comes with knowing that your life purpose is to find the right work and that your work is your offering to humanity. I'm not saying that finding your right work is always easy but the drive gives direction and hope to Generators that often is elusive to the other Types.

Work means different things for different people at different times in their lives. One Generator client was highly successful in creating a business and easily retired in her thirties. Her Sacral Center motor turned to the job of Awakening and she spent endless hours reading spiritual books, watching Mooji videos, doing The Work of Byron Katie. Living in response, she traveled, attended retreats, and followed teachers and teachings that opened her to an extraordinary experience of life. She recently reported that the "Journey is just … amazing. Edges, middle, everywhere really. Katie was right about it all." The inner work of awakening is understood in many traditions as the most potent and generous work anyone can offer.

The Gift of Relational Capacity

Unlike the Manifesting Generators (who have the power of a motor to the throat), the Generator's lack of a motor to the throat creates a vulnerability that becomes a strength. Without the capacity to manifest on their own, Generators are reliant on relationships with others to electromagnetically hook up a motor to the throat. This requires Generators to work cooperatively with others and makes them natural team players. For example, Generators need to either be around a Manifestor or a Manifesting Generator to access their throat, or they need to be around another Generator, a Projector or a Reflector that has a gate that will connect a motor to their throat. This is a bit ahead of us, but as an illustration, I have the whole Channel 50-27 from the Sacral Center to the Spleen Center. I also have the Gate 20 In the Now, which comes off the Throat Center. My wife (and as it turns out many of my clients) has the Gate 57 Intuition. When we're together, we both get a motor to the throat (Sacral to Spleen to Throat), and each of us has a greater capacity to give voice to our intuition.

If you think about Oprah Winfrey, it's clear that her power comes from being in relationship. She uses interviews as her medium. Her fame is not about Oprah out there talking by herself and espousing her views. That would be more the style of a Manifestor. She's in relationship. She's authentically in response to people. That's her power. She built a whole organization to support her, a vast network of people to work with her on her radio and television shows.

UNDERSTAND AND WORK WITH THE GENERATOR'S CHALLENGES

When you work with the Generator client, you will want to keep in mind their limitations and the struggles they may encounter:

1. Lacking a motor to the Throat Center
2. Wait to respond
3. Trusting their Sacral Center as their inner GPS
4. Vulnerable to burnout
5. Energy resources can be hijacked
6. Frustration

The Challenge of Lacking a Motor to the Throat

Sometimes our gifts are also our challenges, and this is the case with the pure Generators (as opposed to Manifesting Generators) who, by nature, do not have a motor to the Throat Center. There are two challenges for the Generator here: the first is learning to wait to respond to something external before speaking or else risk feeling unheard, and the second is a dependency on others in order to step into their power.

In our culture, we're conditioned to believe that we should act like Manifestors: we should be able to speak and be heard and be able to manifest and create at will. Anything less than that points to inadequacy. When a Generator acts like a Manifestor without responding or without waiting to have a Sacral Center *yes* before they speak, they are vulnerable to not being heard and feeling disempowered. If they compare themselves to Manifestors and Manifesting Generators, they can feel deficient and like something is wrong with them.

The first challenge for the Generator then, is to recognize that they are actually empowered by waiting until they're in response to something before they assert themselves. It's a little like Aikido where something external comes towards the Generator and they use that energy to respond. There can be a lot of power in the Generator's response. The learning to wait to respond before speaking takes practice and can be challenging, but as in a game of jump rope, timing is everything. The timing of when the Generator steps in determines if they get to stay in the game or if they lose their turn getting wrapped up by the rope.

In a group, if Generators wait and speak in response to what others have said rather than speaking first, their power is amplified.

As a side note, as I've mentioned my mom was a Manifestor. Growing up, I watched her give speeches about her travels, on her experience as a pilot, as the statewide President of California's Women's Medical Society and Women's Pilots Association. As a Manifestor, my mom entertained and impacted people through her speech, something I could never imagine doing. I felt deficient compared to her capacity. It was only when I became a Speaking Circle Facilitator that I began to recognize that I had my own deeply connected and empowering way of speaking to groups in response to the group that was different from the Manifestor's style.

The second challenge of not having a motor to the Throat Center is again one of those *our wounds are our gifts* kind of situation. We live in a society that holds independence in the highest regard, but the Generator, to reach their full power, needs others to get that electromagnetic motor to the Throat Center.

I have a client who, in response to her childhood wounding, concluded that people couldn't be trusted. Being multi-talented, she was able to do quite well in her professional work; however, it wasn't until she was able to see the impact of this wound and the limitations it created that she began to open up to being more connected to people. In the process, her work went to the next level both in terms of personal satisfaction and financial gain. I keep going back to the dog analogy: think of a dog who gets to play at the park versus one that's left by itself all day long. The Generators need an activity or that energy can turn destructive. I'm picturing a dog left alone chewing up the couch…

The Challenge of Waiting to Respond

Not only do Generators need to wait to respond in regards to speaking, but in all things: food, relationships, jobs, vacations, movies … everything. Generators are not designed to figure things out ahead of time but to be in response in real-time. When Generators bypass the gift of responding, they are not using their design. It'd be like not using your eyes to see. The waiting to respond can be particularly challenging when we are habituated to listening to and following our Head Center. The mind is quick and it's full of ideas. If a Generator follows those ideas, it can be like going into a rat maze. Say a coaching client comes up with the great idea to teach a class. Maybe it is a great idea, but if it's not in response to someone or something it will not have the energy to be supported. The challenge is to be aware of what the Generator is responding to and to listen to the Sacral Center and follow the guidance it provides.

The Challenge of Trusting the Sacral Center as the Inner GPS

This brings us to the next challenge – trusting the Generator's guidance system. When my client from Brazil misplaced the cord of her car's GPS, it made navigating on Maui quite difficult. Many Generators have misplaced that inner cord, so they don't recognize the guidance when it comes. It's an understandable challenge; most Generators were not taught as children to trust themselves. They were not asked *yes/no* questions and supported to follow what arose. It can be hard as adults to shift from the conditioning of following the logical mind to tuning into the Sacral Center response and surrender to the information it provides. This lack of tuning in and trusting can wreak havoc on our lives.

The Challenge of Being Vulnerable to Burnout

When Generators don't follow their guidance system, the Sacral Center's *uh-huh, uh-uh* response, then they are prone to burnout. Yes, the Sacral Center has endless sustainable energy as long as the Generator is harnessing it in response to the *yes*. If a Generator is busy *doing* without that guidance, then the Sacral Center motor overheats or blows out, which leaves the Generator depleted in a healing crisis.

The Challenge of Energy Resources
Being Hijacked

Earlier I spoke of the saying in Human Design that the world is so messed up because there are so many Generators doing what they have a *no* for. Imagine how easy it is for a Generator to override what they know in their gut to do out of fear, survival, approval, validation, love, appreciation, an image, a raise … the list goes on. It's a fundamental leaving of one's self and abdicating living on one's behalf that ultimately sucks the life out of the Generator. Knowing that Generators have abundant energy, people pull on Generators to complete tasks that may not be in their best interest. It's up to the Generator to discern and follow their Sacral Center responses.

The Challenge of Frustration

The Generator is designed to find the right work and master it. When they are not on task, or when they are stalled in the mastery process, they've hit a plateau, then they become frustrated. The challenge for the Generator is to learn to discern if the frustration is a call to shift what they are doing or to hang in and work through to the next level of mastery. This is not always easy to know. If a Generator stays when it's time to go, they risk burnout. If they leave before they've mastered the task, they risk floundering and being unfulfilled. As you understand more aspects of Human Design, you can look to the aspects of the chart for clues.

APPROACHING THE GENERATOR

1. Support the Generator to follow their Strategy – to be in response

2. Respect the Generator's Sacral responses

3. Ask *yes/no* questions

4. If the Generator is frustrated, help them get clear

5. Respect the Generator's capacity, power, and drive to find the right work

6. Know that if the Generator is burned out or unhappy something is wrong

7. Support the Generator to work and be in relationship with others

8. Always take in to account the Generator's Authority

Your best approach to your Generator client is to trust them and help them to trust themselves. Know that they are capable of accessing what's true for them. Hold the image that the universe is in conversation with them, in the present moment showing them options for them to choose from. Ask things like, "Do you want to do this? Or this? Do you need a vacation? Do you need this food? Would this kind of exercise be good for you? Is it time to write your book? Are you ready to move?" The Generator's task is to wait for the universe to speak, listen to their Sacral Center motor's guidance, and then authentically respond. As the Generator's coach, therapist, or team leader, you are asking the Generator to claim their gifts and to acknowledge and work with their challenges.

This gets back to what was originally transmitted to Ra: Human Design is most important for parents to learn to parent their children. If as children, your Generator clients knew their design and were supported to live it, then I wouldn't be writing this chapter. Your job, to some extent, is one that ideally would have been done long ago. A piece of your work is reflecting who your client is, helping them see that, and supporting them to put it into practice. You're here to support them to know and live their design.

Support the Generator to Follow Their Strategy

The Generator Strategy is to wait to respond.

The Generator's task is to wait for the universe to speak, listen to their Sacral Center motor's guidance, and then authentically respond. When Generators can do this, they activate their inner GPS and are guided in life. But, as I pointed out earlier, many Generators aren't aware of this natural gift and have been relying on their minds as their guidance system. Learning to wait to respond involves slowing down, entering the present moment, and trusting their partnership with the universe. I don't mean this in a woo-woo way. It's quite pragmatic. Generators are given signs to follow. You are supporting your Generator clients to retrain themselves to tap into that guidance and trust their responses.

I remember in 1991 when I was trying to decide which internship I was going to take to get my hours for my Marriage and Family Therapy license. In this competitive field, I was fortunate to have been accepted by my top choices. Both were amazing. One was in San Francisco, a cutting edge training center to work with LGBTQ clients where I would be exposed to diverse clientele and teachings. The other was the Women's Therapy Center in El Cerrito, a much shorter commute with some of the brightest therapists in the Bay Area as supervisors. I couldn't decide which one to take. My mind was making lists, going over the pros and cons, desperately trying to make the "best" decision. This was long before I was familiar with Human Design, but

I distinctly remember the moment the decision became clear. I was driving home down Sacramento Street in Berkeley and I asked for a sign. Almost immediately as I stopped at a stoplight, I noticed the car in front of me had the license plate WTC – the initials of one of the programs I was considering. I understand now what happened: my Sacral had a big *uh-huh*. The deal was sealed. I knew unequivocally that was the right choice. Did I miss out on important experiences I might have gained at the other internship? Undoubtedly. Did going to WTC change the course of my life? Absolutely! I ended up working with Ellen Zucker, a remarkable supervisor who became my mentor. Her deep respect for people and her capacity to work within the system while at the same time following a deeper, non-pathologizing truth enabled me to go into a powerful relational paradigm with my clients and gave me space to embrace my unique approach to working with people.

Respect the Generator's Sacral Responses

It is not enough to work with your clients to support them to listen to and follow their Sacral responses, you must also learn to respect their Sacral Center motor responses. This can be more challenging than it sounds. You may have your ideas of what's best for a person. Maybe you're right. Or maybe you're projecting or wanting something from them. If a Generator is going to learn to trust their Sacral Center they need people around them who support that endeavor. It's a learning curve.

I think of it as a practice. You'll see that Generators who've been conditioned to not listen within will be more than happy to put aside their truth to please or appease. If the Generator has a *no* for something and you convince them to override it to meet your need or your picture, there will be a backlash of some sort. Maybe the Generator will get sick or sabotage the situation. Your support in listening to their responses and then honoring those responses helps Generators build trust that this reorientation is a safe path.

I can think of many situations where I've overridden my Sacral responses. As a child, I was trained not to know what I wanted. I'm flooded with examples, but one that stands out as I write this book was the time I told my mom I wanted to be a writer when I grew up. Without skipping a beat she said, "Oh, no, honey, you don't want to be a writer, writers don't make much money." I must have been about nine, and my favorite thing in the world was writing. After enough times of being told that what I wanted to do or eat or wear wasn't good or right, my response, like many children, was to go underground with my desires and question my knowing. This is not to mother-blame. From an adult perspective, I can see my mom had seven children, all of whom she wanted to be independent and successful. In terms of responding to my desire to be a writer, she was giving what she felt was responsible guidance. Had she known that as a Generator, my dharma would be manifest through my right work and that it was dependent on my Sacral

Center guidance, she might have been curious and asked me questions to help me clarify my direction.

It's very easy for Generators to override or neglect their Sacral Center responses until something clicks in and the Generator realizes that it's better for everyone if they tell the truth and live on their behalf. I read an email this morning from Reid Tracy, director of Hay House. He was speaking about Louise Hay and reflecting on what a stickler she was about following her inner guidance. It was the hallmark of her success.

Until the clarity lands for a Generator that their guidance is one of their biggest assets, the path of tuning in to and following that inner GPS demands vigilance and support. It takes a willingness and a kind of surrender for the Generator to honor and trust themselves. It takes people around the Generator to be curious, open, and interested in the Generator's Sacral Center responses to welcome and reinforce the shift. The proclivity to dominate or manipulate people to get what we want is pervasive and insidious. It's based on a lack of trust and discomfort with difference. It comes back to a fundamental lack of trust in the unfolding of the universe.

Ask Yes/No Questions

The best way you can approach a Generator is to ask them *yes/no* questions. It's said in Human Design that Generators don't know what they want until they're asked. Remembering that Generators are in a dance with the universe, the moment you ask the question, you are the universe asking and giving them something to respond to. Let's say a Generator asks you if they should spend money on making a website. Instead of answering for them, the best thing you can do is ask them, "Do you want to spend money on a website?" This begins the conversation. Maybe they don't know. Maybe they feel they should. Maybe they were told it's time to do it. Your job is then to ask them a series of *yes/no* questions until they get clear. The questions can be ones like, "Does this feel like the best timing for you to build a website? Is there a better time? Is there something you need before you can begin that task?" It's a matter of refining the *yes/no* questions until they reach clarity. You get the picture. Your job is to trust that the Generator knows but needs help getting access to their knowing. If they indeed don't come to clarity it is a matter of needing to wait for more information from the universe. Keep in mind that a Generator's *no* doesn't mean the end of the conversation, it's the opening into the next possibility.

Remember that learning to follow the Sacral Center is practice until it becomes clear. You have to take into account that most of us have adaptive behaviors and sometimes we mis-identify an adaptive behavior for a Sacral Center response. The question "Do you want ice cream?" can be met with an *"Uh-huh."* The next question might be, "Does it keep you up at night?" Again, an *"Uh-huh."* "Do you want a good night's sleep more than you want ice cream?" *"Uh-huh."* This is part of the discernment process Generators will have to go through to reclaim their Sacral Center inner GPS.

If the Generator Is Frustrated, Help Them Get Clear

When you see frustration arising with your Generator clients, spend some time helping them see what's going on. Are they hitting a plateau on the way to mastery, or is it time to get out? A good way to do that is by asking *yes/no* questions! Generators get frustrated. They are here to master something, and along the way they hit plateaus. That's a natural part of the mastery process. When things don't go at the pace Generators want or the way they think it should, their response is to get frustrated. Frustration is the signal that the Generator needs to ask themselves (or be asked) if their Sacral is turned off. Do they now have a *no*, when perhaps they initially had a *yes* to whatever work they were doing, the relationship they were in, or path they were on? Or, is this part of the natural process of mastery, and they are stopping out of frustration before they have a chance to fully complete what they initially had a *yes* for? When Generators take the frustration as a sign to stop without discerning what's going on, they lose out on opportunities to grow and get to a place of fulfillment. On the other hand, if Generators dismiss frustration and override their Sacral Center responses, they can chain themselves to debilitating jobs, relationships, and patterns.

Respect the Generator's Capacity, Power, and Drive to Find Right Work

While Generators are in alignment with our culture's value to work, they are generally not taught the importance of being aligned with their work, nor are they taught to follow their inner guidance with finding work.

You are going to want to work with your Generator clients to help them find the right livelihood. This is core to the Generator's wellbeing and satisfaction in life. It is the blessing and the gift they are here to bring. Right work is the Generator's dharma. Doing what they think they *should* be doing won't suffice. Take a stand for them. Generators have a job to do. Honor them and support them in their life-long contribution. When your Generator client has a *yes* for the work they are doing, they will have a hard time not doing it. And, regardless of the kind of work, they will be fulfilling their piece of the puzzle.

Sometimes a Generator might be on the right track, but their work will need tweaking. For instance, if your client is a great recovery coach but is burning out on people relapsing, she may need to look and see what part of that work she is having a *no* to. Perhaps she's complete with people who are just out of recovery and wants to work with people who have done the basic ego stabilization work and are ready for the next level of growth.

If your Generator client is following their Sacral Center, they will have all the energy they need to carry out their work.

Their energy will be well spent and they will ultimately be more enlivened by their output.

Know That If the Generator is Burned Out or Unhappy, Something Is Wrong

On the other hand, if your Generator client is showing signs of exhaustion, they are most likely doing something they have a *no* for and are burning out their Sacral Center motor. They are not trusting and following their inner guidance system. They are overriding their inner GPS. Chances are they are following thoughts, conditioning, or beliefs that they "should" do something that they're not resonating with. It's worth repeating that in Human Design, we say the world is so messed up because there are so many Generators doing things they aren't "on" for. This is an important consideration with your clients. It matters if they're unhappy at work.

Unfortunately, most people are conditioned to go to their heads for answers. While there is wisdom and there is information in the head, it is not a guidance center for any of the Types. Optimally, parents of Generators would have taught their Generator children to trust their *yes* and *no* – to tune into their inner guidance system in all areas of their lives. Since most of your clients were no doubt conditioned to be logical and think things through, the job now falls on you to reparent or realign your Generator clients with their Sacral Motor operating system. For their health and wellbeing, it's crucial that Generators learn to trust their Sacral response!

Once Generators risk trusting themselves and getting back on track with their authentic guidance, their energy will be restored. Remember that your Generator clients don't "need" to go to bed at a certain time; rather, they will thrive when they go to bed after they have exhausted their energy. It's good for Generators to exercise (again, like working dogs!) so they can discharge the build-up of energy and receive the charge that sound sleep gives them.

I find that if I go to bed when my Projector wife does, I don't sleep as well. Projectors need more sleep! Likewise, when I wake up in the morning, my motor is on, signaling it's time for me to get up and go. If I stay in bed with my motor running, it will tire me. She, meanwhile, gets rest from the longer time spent prone.

Support Generators to Work and Be in Relationship to Others

Understand that two aspects draw a Generator to work and be in relationship. The first is the Sacral Center. This is a deeply relational center. Remember this Center is dancing in response to the universe, and a large part of that dance is with other humans. People give Generators something to respond to! Your Generator client is typically well-suited to work in co-operation with others. Think of redwood groves where the roots of the trees create an underground network that supports the trees to grow to enormous heights. You can also think of the analogy of bees working together to create a hive. The world relies on the Generator Types coming together, using their sustainable energy to create structures for humanity.

The second aspect that draws Generators to work and be in relationship is the fact that by nature they do not have a motor to their Throat Center. As a result, Generator systems are electromagnetically looking for people to work with and be around that bring a motor to the throat to empower them to be heard and to create. There will be more on this in chapter 7 on Manifesting Generators. Unlike Manifestors, Generators are not designed to succeed to their highest level on their own through their own push. There are many ways this can be played out for the Generator. It might look like alone activity in a group, like sitting in a café while writing, or being in a studio with other artists while working on your painting. Or, it could look like playing team sports or working as part of a management team.

Take a moment to look at your chart in relation to your client's: if you are a Manifestor or Manifesting Generator you automatically empower your Generator client while they're with you. If you are a Generator, Projector or Reflector look to see if you have a gate that connects with your Generator client's gate giving them a motor to their Throat Center. If this is the case then you'll both be empowered when you're together. This is an entire topic of study, but something worth understanding.

Always Consider the Generator's Authority

There are many aspects in the chart that may influence your Generator client's proclivities within their Type, but first and foremost you must always consider their Authority. For example, while the Generator is all about following the Sacral Center guidance, Generators with Sacral Authority are designed to make spontaneous decisions while Generators with Emotional Authority are designed to track their Sacral Center response over time before they know to go forward or not. When you work with your Generator client, read chapter 12 to understand and incorporate their specific Authority.

FAMOUS GENERATOR: OPRAH WINFREY

I mentioned earlier that Oprah Winfrey is a Generator. Think about this for a moment. She is one of the most powerful women alive, and, as a Generator, she doesn't have that motor to the Throat Center. She works in relationship. Her fame and influence come not from her impact, but from the impact of her being authentically in response to people and situations. She interviews people and responds to them.

Your Generator clients do not have to be hampered by the lack of a motor to their Throat Center. They can transform that vulnerability into a powerful strength.

Other well-known Generators are the Dalai Lama, Albert Einstein, Bill Clinton, Madonna, Carl Jung, Margaret Thatcher, Deepak Chopra, Meryl Streep, and Julia Child.

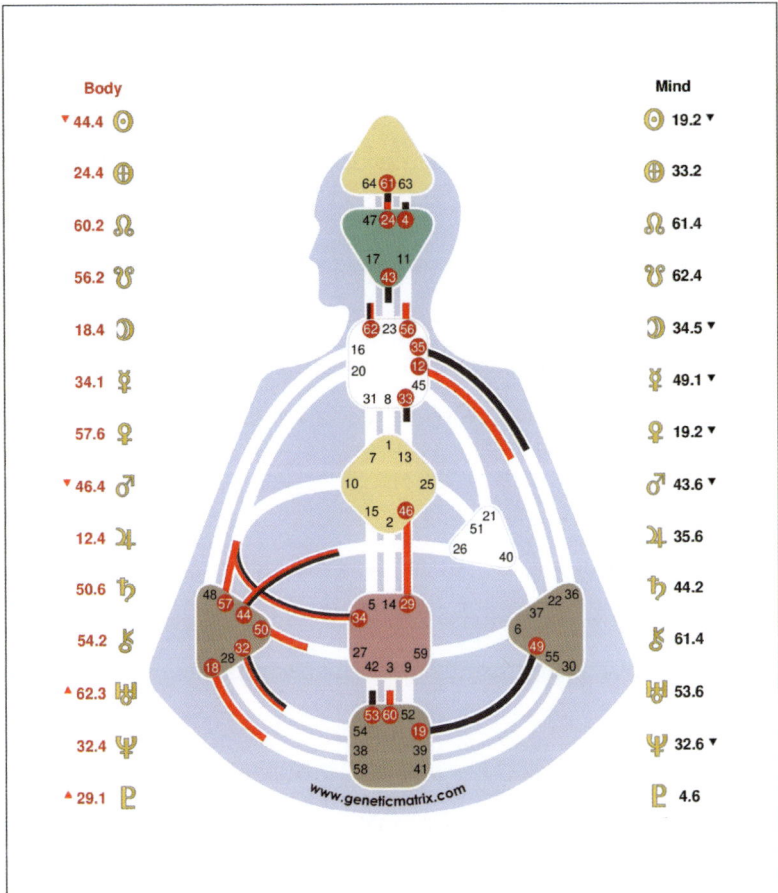

Body

▼ 44.4	☉
24.4	⊕
60.2	☊
56.2	☊
18.4	☽
34.1	☿
57.6	♀
▼ 46.4	♂
12.4	♃
50.6	♄
54.2	⚷
▲ 62.3	♅
32.4	♆
▲ 29.1	♇

Mind

☉	19.2 ▼
⊕	33.2
☊	61.4
☊	62.4
☽	34.5 ▼
☿	49.1 ▼
♀	19.2 ▼
♂	43.6 ▼
♃	35.6
♄	44.2
⚷	61.4
♅	53.6
♆	32.6 ▼
♇	4.6

www.geneticmatrix.com

Type: **Emotional Generator**	Themes: **Satisfaction / Frustration**
Profile: **2/4 - Hermit / Opportunist**	Birth Date (UTC): **29 January 1954, 10:30**
Definition: **Triple Split**	Birth Date (Local): **29 January 1954, 04:30**
Inner Authority: **Solar Plexus**	Design Date (UTC): **03 November 1953, 17:10:33**
Strategy: **Respond**	Birth Place: **Kosciusko, MS, United States**
Incarnation Cross: **RAX The Four Ways 4**	

CHAPTER 8

UNDERSTANDING YOUR MANIFESTING GENERATOR CLIENT

Manifesting Generators are the superhumans with superpowers. They seem to be capable of anything and everything. With their defined Sacral Center, they are first and foremost Generators blessed with seemingly inexhaustible energy and the inner GPS. Added to the Sacral Center is a motor to the Throat Center, enabling Manifesting Generators to be heard, to manifest, and to impact their world. It's as if the Manifesting Generators got the premium package. They are endowed with gifts most of us can't imagine.

Do you have a client that seems to be on the go all the time? Talented? Capable? Extraordinary? Maybe they have ten different projects going at once. More than likely, they are doing them all on their own because it's easier than asking someone else or training someone else. Truly, Manifesting Generators are remarkable.

Earlier, I mentioned that in Human Design we say if this system was a game, you win by getting a motor to the throat.

By these standards, both Manifesting Generators and Manifestors were dealt winning hands. I keep repeating this because it's so easy to compare and judge but rest assured that regardless of how enticing one Type or piece might seem, every puzzle piece matters. Each one counts. We need each one to complete the puzzle. There are benefits and challenges to each Type and design. We can be in awe of the Manifesting Generators and at the same time recognize their challenges and limitations.

Fundamentally, Generators and Manifesting Generators are here to find their right work and master it. Most of what I said in the previous chapter on Generators will also apply to Manifesting Generators, so in this chapter, we'll focus on what differentiates Manifesting Generators from Generators. Please read the chapter on Generators as a foundation for understanding and working with Manifesting Generators

GIFTS PARTICULAR TO THE MANIFESTING GENERATOR

All of these are a result of the motor to the Throat Center, the Manifestor aspect:

1. Being heard and manifesting
2. Impacting people and situations
3. Empowering people
4. Capacity to act on their own
5. Being Prolific
6. Multi-tasking

The Gift of Being Heard and Manifesting

Inherent in the design of a motor to the Throat Center is the capacity to be heard and to manifest. It is through the word that we create, and when our words can be heard, we are empowered and empower others. This is an extraordinary gift; however, it is only activated once the Generator Sacral Center has been turned on. A Manifesting Generator cannot simply think a thought and then speak it, expecting it to be heard. The Manifesting Generator's power comes in response.

When I first began facilitating a Diamond Logos group, one of the participants was a Manifesting Generator. She was on fire about the group and our work. She wanted more time, teachings, and community. Almost effortlessly, as soon as she spoke her desire, she had set up daylongs for me to teach, and she had enrolled people. I watched as she did this in all areas of her life. It was as if, once she was turned on to something, she had a magic capacity to create a structure to support it.

If your Manifesting Generator client is starting a business, chances are that they will be highly successful in promoting it. The caveat here is that the impetus cannot come from an idea; it has to come in response.

My Human Design mentor Karen Curry Parker is a Manifesting Generator. She used to tell a particular story about when she started teaching Human Design. She loved the system and knew it would be beneficial for people. She had the thought of teaching a class. She did everything she knew to do in terms of creating the class. She put up flyers around town, an announcement in the local paper, and rented the space for the class. The day of the workshop, she arrived in full anticipation, ready to share her knowledge.

No one came.

A few weeks later, she was sharing Human Design with someone who said to her, "This is amazing information. People need to know about this. You should teach a class on Human Design." Karen's Sacral responded with a big *yes.* She took the same actions: put the same flyers around town, sent the same announcement to the paper, rented the same space. This time, the class was bursting at the seams. The Manifesting Generator is still in a dance with the universe, responding to cues before their words can manifest.

The Gift of Impacting People and Situations

With the motor to the Throat Center, the Manifesting Generator is designed to impact the world around them. A good example of this is Manifesting Generator, Martin Luther King Jr., the leader of the civil rights movement in the late 50s until his assassination in 1968. In response to racial injustices, he spoke out, his voice was heard, and his speech impacted the course of history. His most famous "I Have a Dream" speech where he passionately implored America to "make real the promises of Democracy" is a call that continues to impact people today.

At a more humble level, I have a client who is a Generator with two Generator children and a Manifesting Generator child. When I was telling her the distinction between Generators and Manifesting Generators, she laughed and said, "We jokingly call my Manifesting Generator son the Little General."

One thing to keep in mind with Manifesting Generators is that while the motor to the Throat Center endows them with that gift of impacting people and situations, their defined Sacral Center dictates a relational, responsive quality like the Generators. For instance, when you picture Martin Luther King Jr., he is not standing alone, impacting the world like a general who is a pure Manifestor: he is in relationship with a movement of like-minded people.

The Gift of Empowering People

The fact that the Manifesting Generator has a motor to the Throat Center means that wherever they are their mere presence empowers those in their vicinity. It's like bringing a powerful crystal into a room. The crystal doesn't necessarily *do* anything; it's emanation impacts people. Everyone around the Manifesting Generator automatically has electromagnetic access of a motor to the Throat center.

Toni Littlejohn, a Manifesting Generator friend of mine, is an incredible artist in Point Reyes, California. For years, she's held art classes called Wild Carrots. It's simple: people come to her studio and paint alongside her. When someone needs help or suggestions, she stops her painting and responds to the need. What's remarkable is that just her presence in the studio elevates everyone's artwork, not to mention the impact of her expertise and guidance when called upon. I've done paintings while working alongside Toni that I never could have done on my own.

The Gift of Having the Capacity to Act on Their Own

We mentioned that Generators need to be around people to get a motor to their Throat Center. Well, Manifesting Generators are connected to people in the sense that their Sacral Centers are in response to people but unlike Generators, Manifesting Generators can and do act on their own because they have a defined motor to their Throat Center. They don't necessarily need other people to help them out. It's often easier for them to do something on their own rather than go through the trouble of telling someone else how to do what they want to be done.

I have a Manifesting Generator friend who is seventy-one years old and the steward of three acres in rural Maui. She cares for the entire property, including two homes, the land, the goats, and the road. She pulls out her tractor and hauls gravel to fix the potholes. She manages the water catchment tanks. She built the houses on the property (with help), procuring most of the materials including blue eucalyptus wood for the counters and redwood for the beams. In addition to caring for the property, until she retired from her job last year as a professor at the University of Hawaii, she has spent a lifetime working towards social justice for vulnerable people, impacting systems to empower people's lives at a profound level.

True to a Manifesting Generator structure, she is *busy*. Always. And multi-talented. I watch her in awe. Her natural inclination is to do work on the land on her own or alongside her best buddy, also a Manifesting Generator. Just as a side note: I do find that Manifesting Generators tend to appreciate each other and be drawn to work on projects together. It's almost like they trust each other to act independently.

On the other hand, she has worked tirelessly with teams of people, heading committees to support students and social justice projects. I've worked with numerous Manifesting Generators who are team leaders. This is a good position for a Manifesting Generator who can act independently, is relational, and can empower and inspire others.

The Gift of Being Prolific

Manifesting Generators can create and create and create and create. They are like geysers that keep producing. To support this abundance of activity, their Generator aspect must be turned on – they must have a *yes* for what they are doing to thrive.

I'll use my mentor, Manifesting Generator Karen Curry Parker, as an example again. She has taught and recorded more classes than any one person could ever listen to. She keeps teaching new classes and offers new material and new information in new ways. She has a full-on *yes* for empowering people to live their authentic lives and she serves endlessly to that end. It's almost inhuman the amount that she has proliferated, and for most of that time, she was a single mom with five kids.

The Gift of Multitasking

Manifesting Generators are busy, they have capacity, and they are typically quick. They can see what needs to be done and do it. This gives them the ability to multitask. This can be a real asset to accomplishing many things.

My friend Gary Bell is a Manifesting Generator. He can concurrently manage a remodel on his home in Inverness, overseeing the design, facilitating the permits, procuring most of the materials, finding the workers, overseeing the project, designing the landscaping, all the while managing a business that includes driving to San Francisco to oversee and fast track permits for builders. It's like spinning several plates in the air all at the same time. Superpowers.

CHALLENGES PARTICULAR TO MANIFESTING GENERATORS

Again, a reminder: please refer to the Generator challenges. These are specific to the Manifesting aspect of Manifesting Generators:

1. Learning to inform
2. Doing everything on their own
3. Being in relationship
4. Lacking focus, skipping steps, burnout
5. Frustration and anger

The Challenge of Learning to Inform

While Manifesting Generators have the Generator challenge of waiting to respond, they have the additional challenge of learning to inform. With the motor to the Throat Center, Manifesting Generators will be impacting people, and they will fare best if they learn to let people know what they are doing. The inclination honestly is for them just to do what they want to do once they have a response to something. They get very absorbed in their projects and forget there is an outside world. This can get them in trouble in relationships with others.

I've had many partners of Manifesting Generators complain about this challenge. Take Gary for example. He can get so caught up in whatever project he's doing, decide to go get something at the store, then be gone for the day without informing his wife. If Manifesting Generators can remember to include the people around them in what they're doing or going to be doing, then things will go much more smoothly. This is also true for Manifesting Generator team leaders. Remember that everyone isn't as quick as you are and will need to be told what's happening.

The Challenge of Doing Everything on Their Own

This is pretty simple. Because Manifesting Generators are so talented and so capable, they can do things on their own. That's the upside we spoke about earlier. But it's also the downside. Again, Gary is a great example. Doing everything on one's own takes its toll. There are times when it's right to get help, and that can be hard for a Manifesting Generator to recognize and accept. As I read these words to Gary, he reminded me to say that Manifesting Generators can easily disregard pain, override their feelings, and miss warning signs...

The Challenge of Being in Relationship

Because Manifesting Generators don't need people in the same way most do, they can be challenging to be in a relationship with if their partner is wanting more time and connection. If their partner appreciates the space or can support their Manifesting Generator partner in being on their own while they're working on a project, then the relationship can work well. But the Manifesting Generator's business and absorption in projects have to be navigated for the relationship to deepen.

The Challenge of Lacking Focus and Burnout

There are a few things to consider here. If the Manifesting Generator is not harnessing their Sacral Center inner GPS, their tremendous energy can be unfocused. They can be very busy doing many things. This has a scattering effect which can undermine the Generator drive to master tasks and ultimately leads to burnout. They can also burn out from not recognizing their limits and overdoing.

The Challenge of Skipping Steps

Because the Manifesting Generator is so talented and so quick with so many things going on, they tend to skip steps. Often this requires going back and redoing something – sometimes at great cost.

The Challenge of Frustration and Anger

Like the Generator, the Manifesting Generator can become easily frustrated when they hit plateaus and have to sort out where their Sacral Center is guiding them. Sometimes their best strategy is to shift directions while at other times they need to stay the course to achieve mastery. The Manifestor challenge is that Manifesting Generators can also get angry when things don't go their way. Think of a superhero getting frustrated and angry. Not pretty. It's almost a knee-jerk reaction and something that Manifesting Generators, if they are to evolve, must learn to work with.

APPROACHING THE MANIFESTING GENERATOR

Again, please read the section on Approaching the Generator and then consider this as an addendum:

1. Support them to follow their Strategy – wait to respond, then inform
2. Respect their wealth of gifts and their superpower capacities
3. Respect their need for undisturbed time
4. Respect that they are designed to be busy and may skip steps
5. Help them to focus their energies
6. Address collapse or burnout
7. Know that they are going to be navigating between independence and being in relationship
8. Understand and work with their frustration and anger
9. Always take into account the Manifesting Generator's Authority

When approaching your Manifesting Generator client, trust that they have big work to do. Don't try to get these clients to slow down. They are designed to be busy, and need to be supported in that – even if it exhausts you to witness their activity! If they are getting tired or burned out, it means they are not following their Sacral guidance. They will need help activating their Sacral response and learning to trust their *uh-huhs* and *uh-uhs*. If they are pushing themselves, they may need to find gentler kinds of busyness to help them relax. Reading, gardening, meditating, something that is at once occupying, but also relaxing is great for them.

Again, you will want to follow the guidelines for Generators (read chapter 7). Manifesting Generators, like Generators, are designed to find their right work. As long as they are following their Sacral response, they have tremendous capacity and talent. If they are not following their Sacral response, they can burn their motor out. Depending on other factors in their charts they might take the stress out on their bodies, or they might fall into a negative mindset. Again, I go back to the working dog analogy: if Generators are working dogs, then Manifesting Generators are the alpha working dogs – they are here to find work they love and master it. They are best when they are exhausting themselves through the right work. In this way, they recharge their batteries and contribute their gifts, making the impact they're here to make.

Like Generators, Manifesting Generators do not know what they want until asked a *yes/no* question. Their proclivity to go to their heads for answers robs them of their inner guidance and wreaks havoc in their lives. Ask them things like, "Do you know what you want to talk about today? Do you know what the issue is that's stopping you from going forward? Are you frustrated and angry?" As you follow a *yes/no* inquiry with these clients, they will get clear.

I had a Manifesting Generator client, who is a coach, recently ask for help regarding which program she should put forth next: an old one she had done before or a new one that was exciting her. You would think from her excitement about the new program that she would have a clear *yes* for it. But that wasn't the case. She was hesitating. As I asked her a series of questions, it became clear that she didn't need to launch a new program right now, even though September was the best time to launch. She wanted to develop the new program but could wait until some things were in place first. The assumption you can make is that your Manifesting Generator client knows but they just need to get in touch with their knowing. And if they don't know, then there is not yet enough information to be clear. They need to wait.

Assume that your Manifesting Generator knows what direction in life they want to go, what would be good for them, and that they can make good decisions. They just may not know that they know until they're asked.

Support the Manifesting Generator to Follow Their Strategy: Wait to Respond, Then Inform

The best strategy for your Manifesting Generator client is to first wait to follow their Sacral response before they take action, then inform the people who will be impacted by their action, and finally to take action. As a Manifesting Generator, Karen Curry Parker has added the step of envisioning your impact after you respond before you act. Because Manifesting Generators can skip steps and have to go back to take care of those misses, the envisioning can be helpful to mitigate that tendency. It also keeps the Manifesting Generator from going in numerous different directions if they have a clear focus, and it keeps them in a relational clarity.

Respect the Manifesting Generator's Wealth of Gifts and Their Superpower Capacities

Never underestimate a Manifesting Generator. Hold them in the highest regard and expect great things from them. Remember they are here to impact and empower people. Support them to do their job!

Respect that Manifesting Generators are Designed to Be Busy and May Skip Steps

Before I was introduced to Human Design, I didn't understand people who were busier than I am. I didn't understand the Manifesting Generator structure.

My dad was a Manifesting Generator. He'd get up at six every morning, take our dog Sheba out for a run, feed the seven of us breakfast, work all day at the hospital, come home for dinner, do some gardening, read his medical journals, query us on our progress at school, go to bed around eleven at night, and repeat. He spent the weekends taking care of the yard, the pool, the house, and car issues when he wasn't at the hospital making rounds or doing emergency surgeries. I thought I was supposed to be like him, but I could never keep up. I've learned to appreciate that that was his operating system.

The skipping steps piece takes different forms for different Manifesting Generators. For my dad, he skipped the step of filing papers and keeping his office clear. He was too busy to take the time. For Gary, he skipped some steps in remodeling his house. Costly steps!

The point is that there is a bit of surrender with Manifesting Generators. You can't make them wrong for skipping steps or try to slow them down. It's part of the pattern that they have to work with and learn to navigate.

Respect the Manifesting Generators Need for Undisturbed Time

With the motor to the Throat Center Manifesting Generators need time to create in an undisturbed environment. Interruptions can throw them off track. Support the Manifesting Generator to inform the people around them that they are taking that time and need space. The informing will help mitigate people around them feeling abandoned and support the Manifesting Generator to care for their needs.

Help the Manifesting Generator to Focus Their Energies

If you see your Manifesting Generator client floundering or going in many different directions at once, help them to focus their energies by engaging their Sacral Center guidance system. Perhaps they are following thoughts about what they *should* be doing. Because they have the capacity, they do all of them but are left unsatisfied. This is not healthy nor supportive for this magnificent Type. It'd be like a fire hose spurting into the street.

If the Manifesting Generator Is Collapsed or Burned Out

Manifesting Generators are designed to have sustainable energy and use it to create. If this is not the case, something is wrong and must be addressed. They are either not following their Sacral Center guidance or they have shut down their empowered motor to their Throat Center. They need your help. Ask them *yes/no* questions to reengage their Sacral Center. If it is their Throat Center that has been shut down through bullying or disrespect, work with your client to empower their voice so they can offer the gift they are here to bring.

Occasionally, you will find a Manifesting Generator who, while quite busy, doesn't feel like a Manifesting Generator but more like an overworked Projector. They feel unheard, unappreciated, and disempowered. This is a curious phenomenon I have seen with some Manifesting Generators who have the Channel 34-20. For some reason, people with this channel can feel particularly overwhelmed and powerless if they are not taking the time to listen and follow their Sacral responses.

Know That Manifesting Generators Navigate between Being Independent and Being in Relationship

Hopefully, it's clear by now that the Manifesting Generator's motor to the Throat Center gives them a level of independence and a capacity to be and act on their own. Meanwhile, their Sacral Center keeps Manifesting Generators in relationship to people. There is a conundrum or a challenge here that Manifesting Generators will be navigating throughout their lives, finding a balance that is comfortable for them. Again, your job is to help them know that this is what they're up against, and there is nothing wrong with them if they have these opposing tensions.

Understand and Work with Their Frustration and Anger

Help your Manifesting Generator client recognize the purpose of their frustration – a sign to help them discern if they need to make a shift, their Sacral Center is guiding them to change directions, or they are stalled at a plateau on the way to mastering something and need to be patient. You will also want to help your client understand and work with their anger response. They get mad when they are thwarted. They're on a trajectory and it doesn't work out the way they planned. Maybe they weren't successful in their creation. This is an opportunity to see the impact they have on people and situations and to slow down and see what's called for in the moment.

Always Take into Account the Manifesting Generator's Authority

Please read chapter 12 to learn about your Manifesting Generator's Authority. This will inform you how they best make decisions while following their Sacral Center responses. For example, if they have a Sacral Authority they can make decisions and act spontaneously. If they have an Emotional Authority they will need to slow down and wait out their emotional wave.

FAMOUS MANIFESTING GENERATORS

Mother Theresa, Martin Luther King, Vincent Van Gogh, Mahatma Gandhi, Madam Curie, Hillary Clinton, Donald Trump, Richard Nixon, Mikhail Gorbachev, Sigmund Freud, Prince, Agatha Christie, and Miley Cyrus.

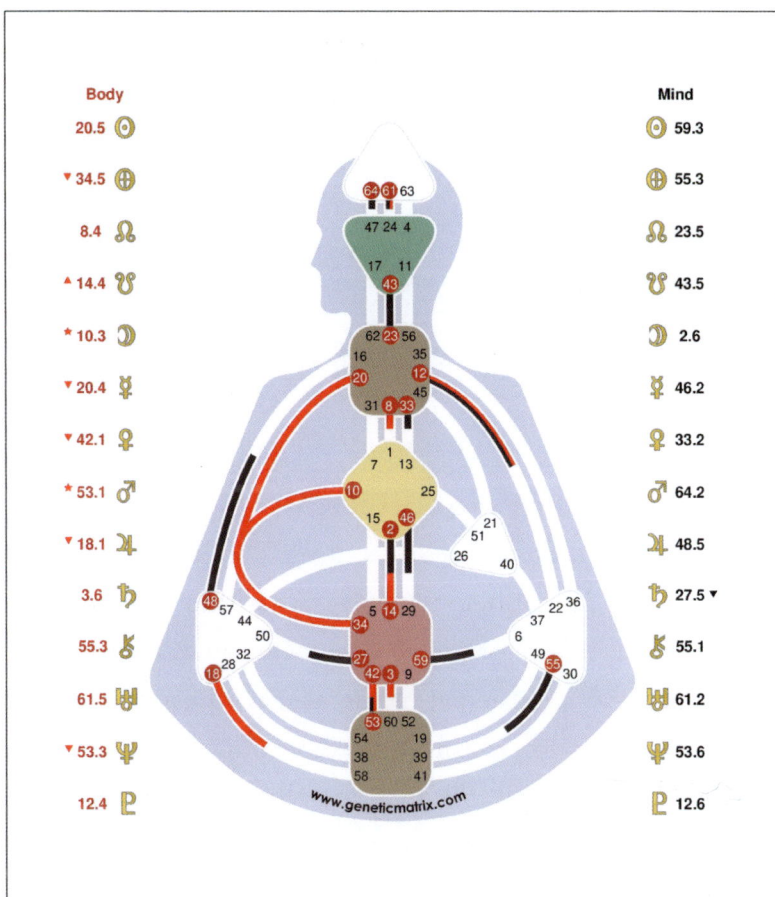

Body

20.5	☉
▼ 34.5	⊕
8.4	☊
▲ 14.4	☋
* 10.3	☽
▼ 20.4	☿
▼ 42.1	♀
* 53.1	♂
▼ 18.1	♃
3.6	♄
55.3	⚷
61.5	♅
▼ 53.3	♆
12.4	♇

Mind

☉	59.3
⊕	55.3
☊	23.5
☋	43.5
☽	2.6
☿	46.2
♀	33.2
♂	64.2
♃	48.5
♄	27.5 ▼
⚷	55.1
♅	61.2
♆	53.6
♇	12.6

www.geneticmatrix.com

Type:	**Pure Manifesting Generator**	Themes:	**Satisfaction / Frustration (Anger)**
Profile:	**3/5 - Martyr / Heretic**	Birth Date (UTC):	**26 August 1910, 13:25**
Definition:	**Single**	Birth Date (Local):	**26 August 1910, 14:25**
Inner Authority:	**Sacral**	Design Date (UTC):	**26 May 1910, 13:42:56**
Strategy:	**Respond**	Birth Place:	**Skopje, Macedonia**
Incarnation Cross:	**RAX The Sleeping Phoenix 3**		

CHAPTER 9

UNDERSTANDING YOUR MANIFESTOR CLIENT

Manifestors have been dealt a powerful hand. With a motor to the Throat Center and an open Sacral Center, they traditionally have held the position of leadership. Their dharma is to initiate and to impact people and situations. A meager 8 percent of the population, these potent people are not designed to be told what to do. They have the envied capacity to speak and be heard. To, well, manifest! Their intense penetrating auras can be intimidating and repelling to people, but at the same time, they can be delightful and inspiring. Even though they are our clients, we can feel dominated, overpowered, or provoked by them. Not dependent on others, they are sometimes called the lone wolf.

Your Manifestor client has the important gift of initiating action. Traditionally, they have held the role of the leaders in society, acting as the generals or dictators, in line with the patriarchal father-knows-best figure. As we shift to a world where the individual is being called into their authority, that leadership role is slowly being turned over to the Projectors as the wise guides. None the less, the Manifestor's role and activity are crucial to the fabric of humanity. In Western culture, we are taught that we should all be like Manifestors. Our voices should be heard. We should be able to make things happen. The self-possessed Manifestors are at once envied and rejected, admired and denigrated. They are an asset in any business as they keep things moving and support products and messages to be heard. Electromagnetically, Manifestors empower anyone who is around them, giving people access to a motor to the Throat Center. Manifestors can do things other people just can't or wouldn't do. They're like the dazzling light of the puzzle. They can move quickly, as most of them are not designed to wait before they take action. In a way, they're like action figures who impact everyone around them.

If you've got a Manifestor in your practice, hold on to your hat, because this is a different type altogether. You have a powerhouse on your hands.

RECOGNIZE AND SUPPORT THE MANIFESTOR'S GIFTS

The gifts of the Manifestor revolve around power:

1. Initiating action
2. Impacting
3. Speaking and being heard
4. Acting independently
5. Leadership

The Gift of Initiating Action

With their defined motor to the Throat Center, Manifestors are specifically designed to initiate action. They get things moving. With their open Sacral Center, they're not necessarily designed to do the follow-through; that task is left to the Generators.

My oldest brother is a Manifestor. As a high school senior, he worked as a river guide. Within a year, he had started his own rafting company, ultimately initiating all six siblings into being river guides. He not only opened our family to the world of rafting, but later ran first descent river trips in China and Tibet and, with his son, initiated some of the first rafting companies in China.

Photo of my Manifestor brother Pete on the left, me, my younger sister, two of my brothers and my parents on a Grand Canyon rafting trip

139

The Gift of Impacting

Not only do Manifestors initiate action, but they also impact people and situations, altering people's lives and the course of events. This can show up in a variety of ways. I recently participated in a training on transformational speaking. The heart of the course was learning to impact people through our authentic stories and (drum roll) call people to action. The inspirational teacher, Gail Larsen, believes that "We each have within us a powerful voice for change." At the close of the course, I asked to run her chart. It will come as no surprise to you that she is a Manifestor and is completely on track with her dharmic duty of impacting and initiating people into action. If you read the testimonials of people who have taken her course, the theme is that it was a game-changer for all the participants.

My trans nephew Finn's life and death tell another story of a Manifestor altering people's lives and impacting the course of events. Finn lived true to his Manifestor nature. Who he was stood out in the small town of Fairfield, Iowa – from how he dressed, to his impressive art, his unusual perceptions, his trans identity – his presence was felt. His impact continued in his death as he ended his life at fourteen, laying on the local railroad tracks. The death of this quirky, wild, deeply loved being had an immediate impact on our family and his community. But it also had an unexpected impact on Iowa politics and gender bathroom regulations, prompting the local public school to abandon their fight to reverse the mandated transgender policies. Newspapers reported that political failures that followed in the wake of Finn's death and the outcry it caused shifted the entire National Republican Party's platform away from using transgender bathrooms as their lead issue.

Finn's large memorial was live-streamed and continues to be shared and watched on Facebook. People have written songs about him and there is a movie script being written about his life. This is a Manifestor at work, living their piece through life and death.

The Gift of Speaking and Being Heard

The capacity to speak and be heard is not only deeply gratifying, but it is also a boon in terms of navigating in the world, finding work, being successful. In marketing and politics, this gift is extremely valuable. As I write this I can hear some of the Manifestors I know protesting, pointing out their fear of speaking and the trauma of not being heard. It's true, for several reasons this gift can be buried or locked away. If you read Gail Larsen's story, she "suffered from a deep-seated fear of public speaking." But this gift is part of the mechanism of being a Manifestor. It's available and could be more active than the Manifestor recognizes. Sometimes the feeling of not being heard is mistaken for people resisting what the Manifestor has to say and the impact the words have.

The Gift of Acting Independently

Of all the Types, the Manifestor is the most independent and the most capable of acting on their own. Because of their defined motor to the Throat Center, they can manifest and create without needing others. Unlike Manifesting Generators who have to wait for a Sacral response, Manifestors can act without advice or input from others. This gives Manifestors great freedom to move about in the world. My Manifestor marketing coach, Amari, calls himself a free spirit. That is a quality I would ascribe to Manifestors.

The Gift of Leadership

The fact that Manifestors have a voice that can be heard and that they are free to act independently places them in the position to lead. There is a self-possessed quality about Manifestors that inspires awe and trust that matters are in capable hands. If you were ever on a raft trip with my brother Pete as the lead boatman, you would feel you were in good hands. Regardless of how big the waves, no matter how bad the situation might look, his innate aura of confidence and his capacity to act quickly created an overall feeling of safety for everyone involved.

UNDERSTAND AND WORK WITH THE MANIFESTOR'S CHALLENGES

The Manifestor is loaded with admirable gifts, and with that comes abundant challenges:

1. Having a power hand

2. Being broken

3. Acting independently – not needing others

4. Repelling auras

5. Needing to inform

6. Not knowing when enough is enough

7. No reliable inner guidance system

8. Not designed to sustain energy

9. Communication needs

10. Anger

Having a Power Hand

Having been dealt a powerful hand is one of the Manifestors gifts, but it is also one of their great challenges. It's a little bit like having wealth – there can be guilt or an embarrassment of riches when so many people feel powerless. I had a Manifestor client speaking to this just the other day. She's in a program where people are making goals, and hers are exponentially bigger than anyone else's in the program. She knows she can meet those goals while others are stretching to reach their own less lofty ones. How do Manifestors use their powerful presence skillfully? How do they act without upsetting people? Is it okay for them to be as big as they naturally are?

Manifestors walk into a room and their big auras automatically impact people. People don't necessarily like being impacted. It creates a bit of an out-of-control feeling, which most of us resist. We envy Manifestor's power and yet can feel dominated by it. Many parents struggle with Manifestor children whose power and audacity naturally unnerves them.

Being Broken

It's not unusual for a Manifestor to be surprised at discovering their design. They don't often resonate with feeling powerful and impactful. Women especially can find it puzzling initially. The misconception of oneself and one's piece is in part a direct response to how a Manifestor child is raised.

Manifestors are perhaps the most challenging children to parent. With their powerful hand, they are not designed to be told what to do. They're independent, self-possessed, impacting, and they take action as they please. Parents react to their child's power and audacity by trying to socialize their children (especially girls). The tendency is to show them who's the boss by dominating and controlling these kids. Like wild stallions, parents set out to break them. This does not bode well.

On the other hand, I've met Manifestors whose power didn't threaten their parents and so they weren't resisted or dominated as children. These Manifestors tend to have striking ease and comfort with their power.

If your Manifestor is not living an empowered life, they have undoubtedly been conditioned to be a different piece of the puzzle than they are. They've most assuredly had their spirit broken. This is a loss for all of us, and a call to redeem and reclaim that lost self.

Acting Independently – Not Needing People

The capacity to act independently without the input of others and to create on their own is one of the Manifestor's gifts, but like the hand of power, it can also be a great challenge. While we admire individuality, we also value connection, and it can be confusing to Manifestors where they fall on that continuum. With their fierce independence, Manifestors are not especially team players. You can imagine this might be a tricky place for Manifestors when they try to work with people who have different opinions or when they have bosses or teachers or parents in the role telling them what to do.

In a way, Manifestors are on their own in the world and are designed to be that way. I had a Manifestor client who believed something was wrong with her because she was happiest being home alone with herself. When we worked with her chart and she understood the Manifestor's proclivity for aloneness, something relaxed in her. She stopped beating herself up. She had permission to freely enjoy her alone time.

I've seen this confusion with Manifestor moms as well. They don't seem to have the archetype of the nurturing mom that our culture idealizes. I experienced this with my mother and struggled with it. What these Manifestors do have is another invaluable gift – the mother bird's inclination to initiate independence by supporting their children to leave the nest and fly on their own.

Repelling Auras

Another challenge that dovetails with the Manifestor's power, the dampening of their power, and their independent streak is their repelling auras. I know that might sound bad, but hear me out. It's simply that the Manifestor's mechanical structure operates from a place of creativity and power that is outward streaming, thus initiating and impacting. So from an energetic standpoint Manifestors are extending energy. They are not receiving energy. You could say they have the role of sperm rather than the role of the egg. This action of moving outward can be repelling to people who do not want to be impacted. People can resist the Manifestor at an energetic level. All of this happens before any words are spoken and often at an unconscious level. The existence of a Manifestor in a room, no matter what conclusions they have about themselves as empowered or disempowered, impacts the room and creates a reaction. Manifestors who may be trying to downplay their power have no control over this phenomenon. They can feel people being intimidated or pulling away and can either take that personally or recognize it for what it is.

Needing to Inform

The best shot Manifestors have in relating to people and having the impact they're desiring is to learn to inform people before they take action. This is not always easy for Manifestors as they fear if they let people know what they're going to do they will be stopped. Here's an example of my brother Pete not informing and losing his job.

In the late 70s, Pete was hired as the first river ranger on the Colorado River. Until that is, he (in his Manifestor way) decided to run the Colorado River with a buddy in kayaks in the middle of winter without informing anyone. To have enough food on the river, since he went without any raft support, Pete had planted hard-boiled eggs at various campsites while on an earlier trip. Had his friend not published a piece about this adventure, Pete might have kept his job. He did not inform anyone because he did not want to be denied the adventure. His behavior was seen as not appropriate for a Ranger.

Not Knowing When Enough Is Enough

The open Sacral creates another challenge for the Manifestor as they take in the Generator energy in the field and do not know when enough is enough. If they don't learn to navigate this, they can risk burnout or be perceived as "too much." They can also overindulge in unsupportive self-soothing behaviors, not knowing when to stop.

No Reliable Inner Guidance System

Manifestors have a particular conundrum because they are not equipped with the inner guidance system of the Generators and Manifesting Generators. They do not have the Reflector's directive of waiting or the Projector's clue of being asked or acknowledged. Manifestors have to throw the spaghetti on the wall and see if it sticks before they know if they're on track. They get a little help from their Authority (see chapter 12), but really, it's not that easy for them. Some of my Manifestor colleagues report that if they can get a body sense of the right timing to take action, things go a little bit better.

I recently worked with a Manifestor in her sixties who was attacking herself for not knowing what was next. As we talked about her being a Manifestor, she let go of the pressure of thinking she should know and opened into the present. She let her curiosity come to the forefront and moved into honoring herself. Being a Manifestor truly takes a level of surrender.

Not Designed to Sustain Energy

Like the other open-Sacral types (Projector and Reflector), the Manifestor has the challenge of not being designed to work or go to school in the cultural nine-to-five norm. They simply do not have that sustainable energy. They do best by initiating a project and then leaving the "footwork" aspect to the Generators. Manifestors need more downtime and rest away from the Sacral motor energy.

When I was telling this to my Reflector friend who has two Manifestor children, she nodded her head in agreement, saying that her son did not do school. It didn't work for him until he found a program where the kids went to school in the morning and they were free to ski in the afternoons as long as they kept their grades at a certain level.

My Manifestor mom was homeschooled until high school, which she graduated in two years at the age of fifteen. Manifestors can move quickly – remember? Homeschooling is a great option for any open Sacral. My Manifesting Generator dad would get up early, jog, come home, wake us up, fix us breakfast, and make sure we had made our lunches while my Manifestor mom would sleep in. She needed her "beauty rest" as she called it. In the afternoons, she'd take her "power naps." Her friends were horrified. This was not what mothers did. Especially mothers of seven children! As a Manifestor, my mom had a chart organizing all of us doing the house chores including doing our laundry by age nine. She instinctively knew that she was not a Generator type. This does not mean she was a slouch by any means. I always thought she had a bigger battery pack than her seven kids put together. What I understand now is that she was taking in and amplifying the seven defined Sacral Centers she was living with. Of course she needed that resting time! As a Manifestor, your clients will have to learn how to manage their energy regardless of the cultural norms.

Communication Needs

Manifestors have a challenge with communication. They need space and time to let their thoughts out. If they are interrupted they can easily lose their train of thought.

Anger

While Generators get frustrated, Manifestors get angry when things don't go their way. Anger is not one of the easiest energies to be around. It's usually repelling. This combination of power and anger can create an unstable atmosphere which can further threaten people. One of your Manifestor's challenges is to learn how to manage and work with their anger.

APPROACHING THE MANIFESTOR

1. Respect their power
2. Understand that they may not recognize their power and capacity
3. Don't try to control them
4. Work with their communication style
5. Understand that they are loners
6. Support them to follow their Strategy – inform before taking action

Respect the Manifestor's Power

Approach your Manifestor client with the same respect you would approach a class 5 rapid if you were river rafting. This Type channels a big, powerful force. The reclaiming of the Manifestor's power and potency will be an important aspect of your work with them. It will involve you tolerating their stepping into their bigness. Of course, this is what we say we want, but when they do, it impacts us and can be unnerving.

Understand that the Manifestor May Not Recognize Their Power and Capacity

As we've mentioned, Manifestors may not recognize their power and capacity. They'll be supported by seeing where and how they naturally have power and impact, as well as understanding how their power might have been shut down and begin the process of reclaiming it.

Don't Try to Control Them

Manifestors truly are independent and self-possessed. Be aware of any tendencies on your part to dampen their free spirit. They are capable of far more than most.

You may notice that people who are around Manifestors can take that Manifestor energy and amplify it, trying to get the upper hand in a situation. I watched this (not pretty) dynamic as my five older brothers tried (unsuccessfully) to take on my mother. Their attempt at dominance was not sustainable, and her natural dominance, which was not a *doing* but rather an energetic way of *being,* always won out. She always had the upper hand. We grew up with the understanding that my mom was the boss, even though my dad was the breadwinner.

Work with Their Communication Style

Any open Sacral person including Manifestors, Projectors, and Reflectors will not do well with *yes/no* questions. Most have been conditioned to believe they are Generators and will go to their open Sacral for a response, but it will most likely be a conditioned response. Better to ask your Manifestor client open-ended questions like "I'm wondering how you feel about asking that person out?" rather than "Do you want to ask her out?" You will want to teach your client to ask the people around them to ask them open-ended questions as well. I've found over and over again with couples that this one slight shift – asking questions appropriate to design makes a huge difference in couple communication.

The other thing you want to be aware of with Manifestors is that they need space to allow their thoughts to flow. If you interrupt them, they lose track of where they were. They have a nonverbal creative process that requires time and space. As a Generator, my inclination is to jump into conversations in response to what a client is saying. I have seriously had to learn to hold back and exercise patience and attentiveness with Manifestors and other open Sacral types.

Understand That They Are Loners

When we talk about Manifestors and relationships, we have to reiterate that Manifestors are not dependent on people the same way the other types who do not have a motor to the throat are. This can be great in relationship – if they are with someone who is also self-possessed and independent, namely other Manifestors or Manifesting Generators. On the other hand, the Manifestor's lack of needing connection can feel like a rejection.

I've had several Manifestor moms as clients, some of whom didn't understand why having a child didn't give them the same feeling of being complete that most of their women friends spoke about. When they learned about being Manifestors, it resonated and they could drop the guilt they felt as well as the feeling that something was wrong with them. Manifestors don't need other people to feel complete – whether it is a spouse, a child, or a friend. They most likely have been conditioned to believe they should, but in reality, they are just fine on their own.

Support Them to Follow Their Strategy – Inform Before Taking Action

The big coaching support you want to consider with Manifestors is to help them learn to inform people before they initiate action. They often just do things, concerned that they will be stopped or not allowed. When they inform, it prepares others for the impact. People still may not like it, but it can soften the jolt. Just remember that the informing is not a matter of negotiating. The Manifestor is going to do what he or she is going to do. They are not asking permission. Unless you are working with the parent of a Manifestor, or a child Manifestor in which case you want to teach the child to ask permission as a precursor to learning to inform.

Whatever you do, don't try to control your Manifestor client. Don't make them wrong. Give them space to find their way. Don't push them. Trust them. Learn to tolerate their big-ness. Help them to see how powerful and impactful they are – just in their being. And help them to see that what they do does and will impact people. Informing is as much for their own sake as it is for the people they're impacting.

The best strategy for your Manifestor client is to inform then take action. This will be crucial to their success, and once they are clear the informing is not a negotiation they will feel empowered and emboldened.

WELL-KNOWN MANIFESTORS

Manifestor yoga master Paramahansa Yogananda came to the United States in 1920 with very little money or connections and proceeded to introduce millions of Americans to medi-tation. He truly impacted a course of spirituality in America bringing Hindu philosophy and teachings to the west, literally initiating masses of people into Kriya Yoga.

Other Manifestors include Frida Kahlo, Maya Angelou, Adolf Hitler, George W. Bush, Susan Sarandon, Mao, Jesse Jackson, and Martha Stewart.

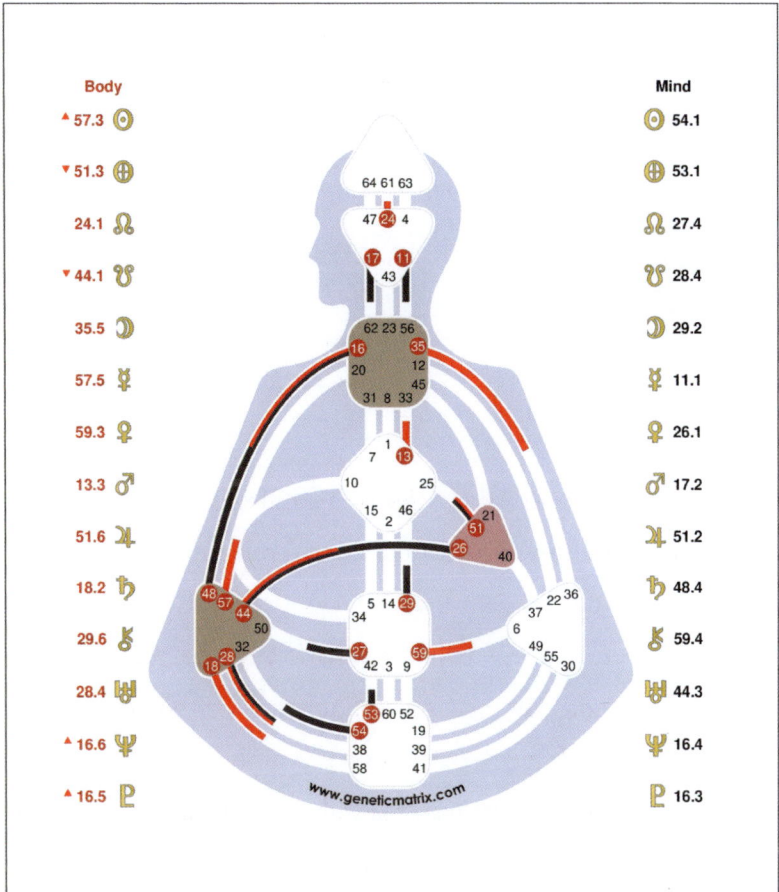

Body

- ▲ 57.3 ☉
- ▼ 51.3 ⊕
- 24.1 ☊
- ▼ 44.1 ☋
- 35.5 ☽
- 57.5 ☿
- 59.3 ♀
- 13.3 ♂
- 51.6 ♃
- 18.2 ♄
- 29.6 ♅
- 28.4 ♆
- ▲ 16.6 ♇
- ▲ 16.5 ♇

Mind

- ☉ 54.1
- ⊕ 53.1
- ☊ 27.4
- ☋ 28.4
- ☽ 29.2
- ☿ 11.1
- ♀ 26.1
- ♂ 17.2
- ♃ 51.2
- ♄ 48.4
- ♅ 59.4
- ♆ 44.3
- ♇ 16.4
- ♇ 16.3

www.geneticmatrix.com

Type: **Splenic Manifestor**	Themes: **Peace / Anger**
Profile: **1/3 - Investigating / Martyr**	Birth Date (UTC): **05 January 1893, 15:08**
Definition: **Single**	Birth Date (Local): **05 January 1893, 20:38**
Inner Authority: **Splenic**	Design Date (UTC): **10 October 1892, 10:23:57**
Strategy: **Inform & Initiate**	Birth Place: **Gorakhpur, HR, India**
Incarnation Cross: **RAX Penetration 4**	

CHAPTER 10

UNDERSTANDING YOUR PROJECTOR CLIENT

Projectors are the hidden jewels in the puzzle. They can go unseen, in which case, their contribution can be unacknowledged. With their open Sacral Center and lacking a defined motor to the Throat Center, the Projector is deeply tuned in to the world around them and wise about people. Not designed to work in the traditional sense, their dharma is to function as guides once they are seen and recognized. Energetically, Projectors are more like cats as opposed to the rambunctious Generator Type working dogs. Projectors are tuned in to the quality of *being* rather than the action of *doing*. With a receptive nature, Projectors take in the energy around them and are guided by what feels good to them. Like a cat amongst dogs, Projectors can be overwhelmed by the excessive energy of the defined Sacral Center that propels Generators and Manifesting Generators to work and to master. As a result, Projectors need space and rest away from the Generator field. Often misunderstood and almost always conditioned to believe they should act and live like Generators, Projectors are vulnerable to burnout and can easily feel undervalued in our culture. Projectors are the future leaders of humanity. If you are aware and recognize them, you will see the gift they are offering and have access to their wisdom.

Once you discover your client – or your daughter, or your spouse – is a Projector, you must know that their life is going to be different than the expected Generator trajectory. Most Projectors I know immediately recognize themselves as Projectors. They are elated to finally be seen and at the same time, they can be distraught by the reality of their type. When I told my twenty-five-year-old computer tech nephew that he was a Projector and wasn't designed to work the way the rest of us were, he burst out, "I knew it!" On the other hand, when I told a client who suffers from an autoimmune disorder that she was a Projector, her response was, "I'm screwed." She was depressed for weeks, realizing that her low energy was a lifelong reality and not something she could recover from. It didn't help that her uninformed Generator husband was constantly demeaning her for her lack of energy, expecting her to be productive. It took time before she could fully embrace and value her piece.

I happen to be married to a Projector. We've been together for thirty-eight years. I've come to have a particular fondness and full-on awe for this unusual, often misunderstood, and, more often than not, undervalued type. I hold Projectors in high esteem. They are precious gems and have an important role to play. They have a particular gift they're offering humanity that requires some sophistication and restraint on their part. They've often been given a bad rap. If you have a Projector in your clientele or your intimate circle, I invite you to explore getting to know them anew, seeing them for who they are and opening to receive the unique presence they have to offer. If you're the parent of a Projector child, know that seeing them matters exponentially. If you are a Projector, I'm hoping this information will invite you to differentiate yourself from any Generator conditioning you might have identified with and welcome your exquisite piece of the puzzle as crucial to the picture.

RECOGNIZE AND SUPPORT THE PROJECTOR'S GIFTS

1. Quality of being
2. Magnetic
3. Strategic maturity
4. Wise guides of humanity
5. Leaders of the future

The Gift of a Quality of Being

With their open Sacral Centers and without a motor to the throat, Projectors have a particular quality about them that is an offering in and of itself. It's a bit tricky to put your finger on.

Their impact comes initially from the quality of their presence. Imagine how an orchid shifts the energy in a room. Think about the quality of a cat moving through without disturbing the space. It's a quality of being at rest and being observant at the same time. In a world of activity, Projectors are tuned into being and aware of what's happening around them.

The Gift of Being Magnetic

When Projectors are honoring their structure and allowing themselves to be in that open, witnessing capacity they are naturally magnetic. When they are not trying to assert themselves or their wisdom, people turn towards Projectors and want what the Projector has to offer. It is this effortless attraction that draws attention to the Projector so they can follow through with their dharmic task of sharing their wisdom and guiding people.

The Gift of Strategic Maturity

To draw in the right people and situations, Projectors must *work smarter, not harder.* When Projectors utilize it, they have the gift of waiting for the right timing, in a self-possessed sort of way, knowing what invitations are good for them to accept and when to strategically share their pearls.

The Gift of Being the Wise Guides of Humanity

With the Projectors observing the quality of being and with their magnetism and strategic maturity, comes the gift of guiding humanity through wisdom and not force.

One of my favorite wise guides is my Projector mentor, Anat Baniel. Anat was extremely fortunate in that her father saw, understood, and respected her from an early age. In her early twenties, Anat studied with Moshe Feldenkrais who recognized Anat as his protégé and invited her to work alongside him. With Moshe, Anat began giving lessons to Elizabeth, a thirteen-month-old child who was diagnosed with global brain damage. From all medical standpoints, the future looked bleak for Elizabeth. However, Elizabeth's parents again recognized Anat and trusted her. Over several years, Anat's patience and her understanding of the impact movement has on the brain coupled with her exquisite awareness of and sensitivity to Elizabeth helped guide Elizabeth to the miraculous life she leads today. Married and with two advanced degrees, you would never know that Elizabeth's slight unsteadiness while moving is the remnant of a life that was headed for lifelong institutional living.

Anat, meanwhile, has been recognized by some of the greatest neuroscientists of our time and has partnered with Michael Merzenich and Jill Bolte Taylor to bring to light a shift in our understanding of how to engage the brain through movement and awareness and the far-reaching implications of doing so. As a wise guide, Anat's NeuroMovement teachings are changing the trajectory of the life of limitation as we have known it.

The Gift of Leadership

It follows that if one is a wise guide, they would be well suited for leadership. In the past, we have looked to the powerful voice of Manifestors to be our leaders but from the Human Design perspective, we say that paradigm is shifting and that it will be the Projectors who become our wise leaders. JFK, Nelson Mandela, and Barack Obama are all Projectors. You can feel the difference in the way they lead from a Manifestor oligarch like Adolf Hitler or Chairman Mao. The Projectors don't take power; they are magnetic.

UNDERSTAND AND WORK WITH THE PROJECTOR'S CHALLENGES

1. Not having sustainable energy – vulnerability to burnout
2. Needing rest
3. Needing space from the Generator field
4. Needing to be in the right location to get the right invitations
5. Needing to wait for recognition or to be invited
6. Struggles with being seen and heard
7. Bitterness
8. Not knowing when enough is enough

The Challenge of Not Having Sustainable Energy – Vulnerability to Burnout

Perhaps one of the biggest challenges a Projector will face is a lack of sustainable energy. While the Sacral Center takes in and amplifies all the Sacral energy around it, thus appearing to have more energy than anyone, they will eventually burn out. Burnout is a major challenge for Projectors and can complicate everything from work to parenting to finances. Without a defined Sacral Center, Projectors are not designed to work nine-to-five, much less as children go to school in the eight-to-three system we've established as the norm.

Projectors are challenged to find work that is copacetic to their operating system. Being a consultant or counselor are examples of good tracks. My brilliant Projector friend Heidi explained to me how she naturally set up her architecture business so that she would meet with clients, then work on her own at home in her own time.

The Challenge of Needing Rest

This brings the question of rest to the forefront. We live in a Generator world where *doing* is the norm and the need for sleep and rest is often brushed to the side. Projectors who are conditioned to think they are Generators will act as if they have sustainable energy and risk burnout. Projectors can't afford to not rest. They need to go to bed before they are tired and sleep until they are well-rested. Often, Generators don't understand this need and can demean or dismiss the Projector's need for rest as laziness. I know. I'm now embarrassed to say that I did this to my wife for years until I learned Human Design! We often judge what we don't understand. As we come to understand each other, we can support our differences.

The Challenge of Needing Space
from the Generator Field

The Projector's open Sacral Center is constantly bombarded by Generator energy. To get the rest they need and to diffuse the Generator rev from their systems, Projectors need to get away, have their own space, and be alone. This sometimes means sleeping separately or taking space from their children. This requires that the Projector recognize and honor who they are and what their system needs. Again, this is not always easy to reconcile say in a work environment, but it's something for the Projector to seriously consider.

If you want a plant to thrive you're going to think about the amount of shade or sun it needs, the amount of water it requires. The Projector can thrive in the right conditions – if they're met. But first, they have to know and understand those conditions.

The Challenge of Needing to Be in the Right
Location to Get the Right Invitations

One of the important conditions for Projectors is the environment or place. Projectors need to be in the right place to get the right invitations. If a Projector is living in a city or home or working in an office that is not enjoyable to them, they won't be seen and recognized. Their magnetism won't be activated. They definitely won't thrive. They'll most likely droop. They won't get the clients or jobs or relationship offers that are waiting for them. In this case, the Projector suffers and everyone else misses out on the gifts they are here to bring.

The Challenge of Needing to Wait for Recognition or to Be Invited

Not only do Projectors need the right environment, but they also have the challenging task of waiting to be seen, recognized, and invited. We're conditioned to think we are Manifestors. We should go out and get what we want, whether it's the job or the relationship. Yeah, that just doesn't work for a Projector operating system. Projectors have to be relaxed and open and enjoying themselves, doing what they love before they are seen. Then they are magnetic. I've never heard this or seen this written, but the way I've experienced Projectors is that they have to be focused on themselves and caring for themselves before they are called into service.

In relationships as in jobs, it's best if the Projector is invited into the relationship. My techie Projector nephew I spoke about earlier was set up on a blind date with a Projector he then married. This is a great way for two Projectors to meet; both were invited into the relationship.

Struggles with Being Seen and Heard

Like the challenge of waiting, the experience of not feeling seen or heard and the attempts to be seen and heard are tough. They often can't figure it out and easily conclude that something is wrong with them. They don't realize that they can't just muscle through; they have to learn that strategy piece.

I have a Projector client who is a brilliant coach. She's smart, sensitive, articulate, deeply intuitive, and able to stand in the fire with people. She's truly amazing. I have never watched anyone work harder to market themself and get less back for their efforts than she has. Honestly, she ran circles around me. I thought for sure when I did her chart that she was a Generator. But as I sat with her very open Projector chart, it made so much sense. She had an off-the-mark strategy of trying to insert herself. She was always almost desperately trying to be seen and known. This is a problem.

Here's the thing: when Projectors are trying to be heard and seen, it's off-putting. It can be abrasive. We tend to reject what they're saying, no matter how wise, because of the needy, distorted place it's coming from. A large portion of her efforts fell on deaf ears. As she explored being a Projector, she began to slow down and rest more. She stopped beating herself up for her failures to be like other people. She started valuing herself more. As she relaxed and "did" less, she became more magnetic. She started being acknowledged and her business increased.

Not trying to be seen or heard is very counter-intuitive in our culture, though it does align with the prosperity teaching on resonance and magnetism. When a Projector learns and embraces their nature and values *being* enough, they gain certain security, peace, and wisdom enabling them to access their gifts and attract those who are available to recognize them.

There's one more curious piece I want to mention here. A Projector can be wildly acknowledged by some and unseen by others. Take the example of Projector Barack Obama who was passionately embraced by the Democrats and recognized as a groundbreaking leader throughout the world to the point of getting the Nobel Peace Prize. On the other hand, he was never really recognized by the Republican Party. It's striking how ineffective he was in his sincere efforts to cross the divide. Likewise, Projector Princess Diana was beloved worldwide, but within the royal family, she remained unseen, unheard, and unacknowledged.

I'll briefly mention a similar story about Anat. You have to know that Anat is a genius. I put her up there in the category of Einstein in her field. In many ways, she and her work are recognized worldwide. In this story, Anat was with a group of powerfully recognized leaders, one of whom had hurt her back. Knowing the miraculous results Anat can facilitate with limitations that show up in the body, several people recommended that Anat help this person out by giving her a session. Anat kindly agreed. Well, this beloved-by-many, powerful, female leader did not recognize Anat. She treated Anat as if she was a masseuse giving her a massage. With no disregard to massage and bodywork, the work Anat does is off-the-chart; it's a new paradigm – it's brain work. It'd be like asking Einstein to bring you a cup of coffee. When you can't see who the Projector is, you can't receive the amazing gifts they have to give.

Bitterness

When the Projector is not seen, heard, recognized, or invited, they become bitter. After all, they are sitting on a gold mine but no one can see that. This bitterness is the opposite of that place of self-care, of feeling joy, of relaxing and trusting themselves. It's not at all magnetic or attractive and exacerbates the repulsion. It's a quality that Projectors need to work with and monitor as it doesn't get them what they're after.

The Challenge of Not Knowing When Enough is Enough

In closing with the Projector challenges, I just want to circle back to the open Sacral Center that is taking in the Generator energy and amplifying it. One of the hazards here and a big lesson for the Projector is that they have to learn when to stop. They don't know when enough is enough. When they try to match and amplify the Generator energy, it can push people away if they don't stay connected to themselves. It can be like a runaway train. You can easily see this in Projector children who are trying to get attention and can't let it go or children who get overwrought and can't wind down. Perhaps you've seen this in adults during a team meeting where someone won't stop talking. They don't get the cues that what they're saying is not being heard. Or, if they get those cues, they try harder by being louder or more insistent. Frankly, it's not becoming to the dignified Projector to lose it like that. It's so important for Projectors to be strategic rather than forceful. That's where the rubber meets the road for them.

APPROACHING YOUR PROJECTOR CLIENT

I am always excited when I can share with someone that they are a Projector. In my experience, Projectors get so little real reflection, often having a lifetime of struggle around being seen and heard that learning their Type is most often a game-changer for them. The feeling that something is wrong with them gets seen in a new light. Their lives make sense in a way that it hadn't before. Shame and self-judgment are replaced by compassion and understanding. There is nothing wrong with them; their role is just terribly misunderstood. I make a point to reaffirm how important their piece is and acknowledge that it is not, for the most part, recognized.

When you bring this perspective to your Projector clients, you have an opportunity to powerfully and quickly change the narrative they hold of themselves and create the opening for a dramatic paradigm shift. It's a whole new world.

1. Start with the assumption that you are in the presence of someone of great value

2. Support the Projector in following their Strategy – wait to be invited

3. Respect what they have to say

4. Reorient your question process

5. Support them to get respite

6. Understand the challenges they face in the work world

7. Always consider the Projector's Authority

Start with the Assumption That You Are in the Presence of Someone of Great Value

I can't stress enough that the biggest support you can offer a Projector is to see that they are a valuable being. Be curious about them regardless of their output in the world. Do not fall into the trap of believing your Projector should be more productive or is lazy. Be open to who they are and the jewels they are offering.

Support the Projector in Following Their Strategy – Wait to Be Invited

The strategy for the Projector is to wait to be invited or acknowledged before they offer their wise guidance. The coach-client I spoke of earlier had to learn to wait and not insert herself, instead to allow people to recognize her and seek her out. This is a big shift for many projectors. Feeling their difference and in an attempt to be seen and heard, they often struggle with inadequacy. They're in a catch-22: they know they are special but they have to wait for that reflection from outside before they can share their wisdom and offer their pearls.

This particular Strategy is not the norm in our culture and at first blush seems a bit passive and disempowering. I remember the first story I heard Karen Curry Parker tell about a Projector client of hers who had been invited to be on a prestigious board. Each month, she was to be flown to New York, put up in a high-end hotel, and given a generous food budget. All she had to do was attend the board meeting. Being a conscientious person, she did all her homework and preparation for the first board meeting only to discover that she couldn't get a word in edgewise. No one seemed to care about what she had to offer. This puzzled her at first, but she let it go. This pattern continued for the next few board meetings and she was beginning to feel like she didn't belong and that she wasn't of value. She consulted with Karen, who suggested she go to New York, have a blast while she was there, and not say a word during the meetings – to simply wait until she was invited. The woman followed this advice and the months went by ... five, six, seven months without a word. In the eighth month, someone turned to her and asked her what she thought. She pulled out her charts and her information and shared her wisdom. The room went still. They listened in awe to her insights. She was consulted at every board meeting that followed.

In a way, she was passive and disempowered when she was trying to be heard. Once she stopped trying to be seen and heard, she entered that mature strategic zone. In our culture, we seem to misunderstand the power and potency of silence and how loudly conscious silence speaks. When Projectors wait until they are invited to share their wisdom, they protect against the tendency to throw pearls to swine and end up feeling bereft.

I've heard it said that Projectors only need to wait for the invitation or to be recognized for the big item things like jobs, moves, and relationships. I see that the more comfortable a Projector is with themselves, the more self-possessed and magnetic they are, then the invitations and acknowledgments are naturally woven into their everyday lives.

Just because a Projector gets an invitation doesn't mean it's a good invitation for them. That is another piece of discernment. The invitations have to feel good to the Projector.

Respect What They Have to Say

Your best shot at accessing a Projector's gifts is to listen to what they have to say. In my therapy practice, I was under the assumption that I was the wise guide and people were looking to me for guidance. When I brought Human Design into my work, I shifted my approach. I became more of a listener, especially for my open Sacral Center clients. Together, we worked with creating space for them to hear themselves and access their knowing.

Reorient Your Question Process

With the open Sacral Center, *yes/no* questions are not useful. The Projector will merely go to a conditioned response for an answer. You will want to ask Projectors open-ended questions and support them to educate the people around them to do the same. It takes practice to say, "I wonder what your thoughts are about going to the movies?" Rather than the Generator questions, "Do you want to go to the movies?" Instead of, "Do you like your work?" Better to say, "I'm wondering what you feel about your work." This will give the Projector the space to open into the question. You will find the Projectors will appreciate and be relieved by this simple shift.

Support Projectors to Get Respite

Let's be clear, a major issue with Projectors is burnout. They must organize their lives around self-care. For Projectors to function well, they must feel joyful and good and easy in their bodies. Stress is a killer for everyone but especially Projectors. We have a lot to learn from Projectors about ease and effortlessness. If you remember that Projectors aren't here to work in the same way that Generators are, that it is not their dharma, then you can back off of the cultural pressure for them to produce and make space for their wisdom.

Understand the Challenges the Projector Faces in the Work World

There are special considerations with Projectors that are important to hold in mind concerning work and finances. You can assume that your Projector would do well to have financial support or build large savings for their retirement. As a Generator, I can imagine working until I die. This is not true for Projectors. Many projectors (not all, of course), struggle financially. In their early adulthood, many Projectors mistakenly try to act like Generators. Unless they are tuned into themselves and honoring their needs, they often start to burn out in their early thirties. The best kind of work for Projectors is some kind of consulting work where they are guiding others. A job where they are recognized will empower them, while a job where they are not seen can be devastating, leaving them bitter. Even the act of getting a job is tricky for a Projector. The best jobs for them are ones that they're invited into.

If you're supporting a Projector client with their marketing materials, you'll want to encourage them to keep the focus off of themselves. They'll be more magnetic if they have a small picture of themselves rather than feature themselves. The less they talk about themselves in their copy, the better. Again, it may sound counterintuitive, but with Projectors, the more they try to be seen and show up, the less they are seen. The more they rest in themselves from the witnessing vantage, the more they will attract the attention of others. Likewise, their copy should include an invitation for people to join them.

While there are Projectors who struggle, there are also Projectors who have mastered this path. I think of my friend Lucia Maya as my poster Projector. She's clear on her limits, honors her need for rest, doesn't overwork, and does her Reiki healing sessions from home, often by phone. She has a passive income from a rental and gets referrals from a functional medicine doctor who sees and values her. She is not depleted or bitter. She's an empowered Projector.

Always Consider the Projector's Authority

As with all the Types, you must include the Projector's Authority when you support them to live their piece. A Projector who has Emotional Authority, for example, would need to take more time feeling the rightness of an invitation than a Splenic Projector. See chapter 12 to include your client's Authority in the mix.

The thing to keep in mind about Projectors is that they thrive when they feel good at a being level. Again, think about cats. These luxuriating, leisure creatures are not "doers" their gift comes from their capacity to *be*. When a Projector comes into alignment with themselves and surrenders to their path (i.e., when they stop trying to do and move into their witnessing power), their very presence is a transmission. To be around them relaxes our system. It's like having flowers in your home. Their presence and beauty shifts the energy. Once they are invited or acknowledged, they can speak and be heard in a way that makes people listen. Projectors bring wise counsel that is worthy of considering.

WELL-KNOWN PROJECTORS

In addition to Princess Diana, Barack Obama, Nelson Mandela, and JFK, other famous projectors include Queen Elizabeth II, Osho, Barbara Streisand, Liz Taylor, Woody Allen, Denzel Washington, Ramana Mahrishi, and Sri Aurobindo.

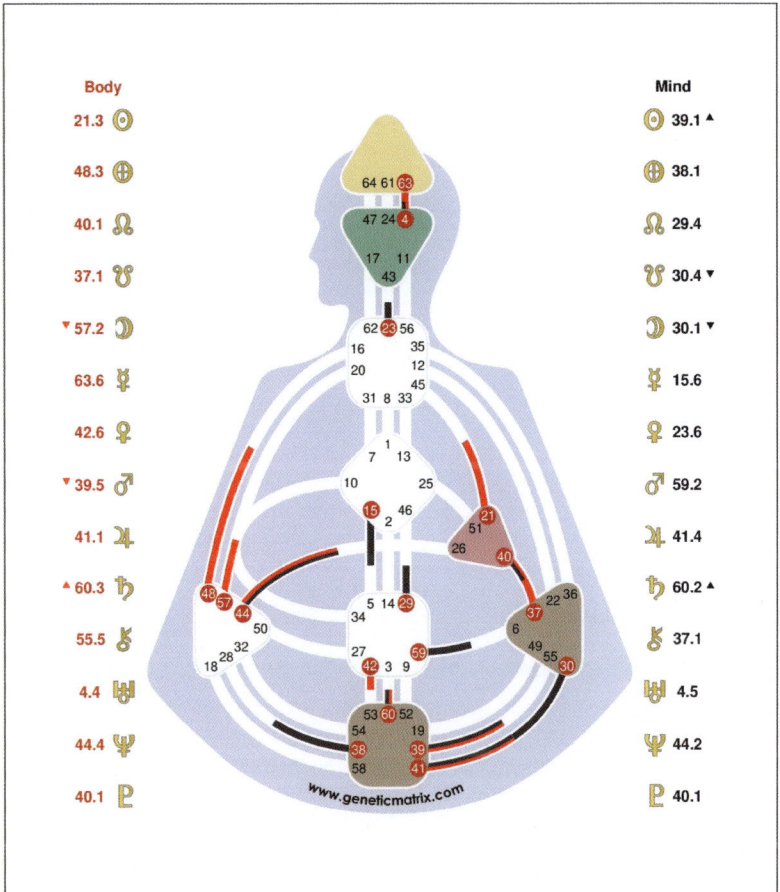

Body

- 21.3 ⊙
- 48.3 ⊕
- 40.1 ☊
- 37.1 ☋
- ▼ 57.2 ☽
- 63.6 ☿
- 42.6 ♀
- ▼ 39.5 ♂
- 41.1 ♃
- ▲ 60.3 ♄
- 55.5 ⚷
- 4.4 ♅
- 44.4 ♆
- 40.1 ♇

Mind

- ⊙ 39.1 ▲
- ⊕ 38.1
- ☊ 29.4
- ☋ 30.4 ▼
- ☽ 30.1 ▼
- ☿ 15.6
- ♀ 23.6
- ♂ 59.2
- ♃ 41.4
- ♄ 60.2 ▲
- ⚷ 37.1
- ♅ 4.5
- ♆ 44.2
- ♇ 40.1

www.geneticmatrix.com

Type:	**Emotional Projector**	Themes:	**Success / Bitterness**
Profile:	**1/3 - Investigating / Martyr**	Birth Date (UTC):	**01 July 1961, 18:14**
Definition:	**Split - Large**	Birth Date (Local):	**01 July 1961, 19:14**
Inner Authority:	**Solar Plexus**	Design Date (UTC):	**01 April 1961, 14:54:00**
Strategy:	**Wait for Recognition and Invitation**	Birth Place:	**Sandringham, United Kingdom**
Incarnation Cross:	**RAX Tension 2**		

CHAPTER 11

UNDERSTANDING YOUR REFLECTOR CLIENT

Reflectors are magical beings. Sometimes spoken of as karmic mirrors, Reflectors are the canary in the coal mine – here to reflect the health and well-being or lack of health or well-being in their community.

But who are they really?

That's a good question and one that is not easy to explain. Reflectors have all 9 centers completely white, totally undefined. This means they don't have consistent access to any of those 9 centers that the rest of us rely upon to have some sense of self and grounding. Reflectors are profoundly fluid beings. They are taking in and amplifying the energy around them on all levels. They function like mirrors to the people they're around. They are not designed to be consistent in their thinking, processing, speech, identity, values, or energy. They are also not designed to be consistent in relationship to fear, intuition, their emotions, or their adrenalized-spark to take action. Every day, they are different depending on who they are around and the current planetary transits. In Human Design, we call them lunar beings: because of their openness it's said they need to wait for a full moon cycle before they make important decisions. Less than 1 percent of the population, Reflectors are so radically different from the rest us that it's hard to comprehend or fathom who they are and how they operate.

In Vedic inquiry, *neti neti* is a Sanskrit expression that means, "Not this, not that." I'm neither this nor that. Reflectors are all things and nothing. Realizing and living their Type requires opening to and grounding on their complete utter transparency. In surrendering to their self, which is all or everything, they fluidly meet what's in front of them. We could say that when Reflectors are healthy and living their design, they have a natural connection to awakening. When they are unhealthy, there are two possibilities: either they have been unable to tolerate their openness and have grounded on the conditioning of those around them, creating a kind of rigid structure that enables them to survive, but not thrive, or they are in a community that is unhealthy and reflecting that lack of health back. Their work is either to release their identifications or to change their location.

RECOGNIZE AND SUPPORT THE REFLECTOR'S GIFTS

1. Clear mirrors

2. Fluidity

3. Oneness with nature

4. Knowledge

5. Connected to all things – awakening

The Gift of Being Clear Mirrors

Reflectors hold a particular piece of the puzzle – the piece that mirrors us back to ourselves. Being in their presence requires us to look at ourselves in full light without barriers. They are here to let us know if we are being authentic or out of alignment with ourselves. Reflectors have the capacity, like a clear mirror to be non-judgmental observers reflecting what they see.

A parent with a Reflector child recently reached out to me. She spoke about how challenging it was to parent her son. He continuously reflected every detail of herself back to her. From her hairstyle to her clothes to her mood, he saw and reflected it all. She was clear that he was her teacher. She couldn't get away with anything around him. While his constant mirroring was unnerving, it also forced her to grow in ways she welcomed and was grateful for. She described it as the hardest and the best thing in her life.

A Reflector friend of mine is a therapist. Like the parent I mentioned above, the clients she attracts have to be ready for a transformation. When they work with my Reflector friend, it's like they enter an intensive reflective vortex where they are seen and have no room to hide. My friend's wife says that being in partnership with a Reflector is a continual process of being shown herself.

Another Reflector friend, David Groode, is an extraordinary intuitive. His openness enables him to see and reflect what is hidden to most of us.

While this gift of being mirrored hits upon our ego structures and brings a level of disorganization to our self-image, it is also what we most want, it is nectar to our souls.

The Gift of Fluidity

This is one of those gifts that is also a challenge. With all 9 centers open, the Reflector is free to meet every moment new. This means they meet themselves as new in each moment as well. Who they are shifts depending on the current location of the planets, the people they are around, and the physical location they're in. It can be a bit hard for the rest of us to fathom this chameleon-like self that is in continual flux. It almost has a quantum physics or sci-fi feeling to it. This fluid nature gives Reflectors the capacity to meet all varieties of situations without preconceptions enabling them to truly be present at the moment.

The Gift of Oneness with Nature

When I speak to Reflectors, a consistent theme I hear is their profound connection to nature. Many of them speak of nature as the thing that saved them as children. In a world where Reflectors were so different from the other humans, nature was like a mirroring parent to them, nourishing them, reflecting back to themselves more accurately than people did. The experiences of nature that Reflectors share can sound almost shamanic as they easily merge into Oneness with nature and experience it from dimensions most of us don't have access to.

The Gift of Knowledge

I have never heard this taught or seen this written anywhere, but it makes sense to me and it's been my experience across the board with Reflectors. With all their openness, Reflectors often turn to knowledge to find a sense of ground and to interface with the world. Reflectors understand the world through gaining knowledge. It seems to stabilize them. They often have multiple degrees or certifications. More than one Reflector I've known has a photographic memory. The best way I can understand it is that there isn't anything between them and knowing information and systems. Maybe it's like whatever they put in front of themselves they absorb?

The Gift of Being Connected to All Things

With all their openness, Reflectors have the easiest access to the spiritual experience of living in Oneness or perhaps being Oneness, the experience of Awakening. When Reflectors are living their design (in other words not identifying with conditioning), all their open centers, their portals to God (the Universe – whatever your word would be) are available. Lacking fixed definition in their centers renders them invisible to others. This invisibility can act as a support for what I've consistently seen as their unusual and understandable spiritual devotion. They have access to the whole of life in a way that many people can't imagine. Let's be clear, their dharma involves being and reflecting the Oneness.

UNDERSTAND AND WORK WITH THE REFLECTOR'S CHALLENGES

1. The lack of bearings
2. The need for the right environment
3. Living in a pressure system
4. Not knowing when enough is enough
5. Need for rest and to be out of the projection field
6. Appearing invisible
7. Wait for a full lunar cycle before making decisions
8. Disappointment

The Lack of Bearings

With all their openness, your Reflector client doesn't have the bearings the rest of us rely on for identity. This challenge is compounded by being so different from the majority of humanity that the Reflector doesn't have role models or people mirroring them. The Reflector's variability can be disorienting both for themselves and the people around them. Their fluidity can be crazy-making for everyone. The answer to the question *Who am I?* changes moment to moment, and until the Reflector learns to rest in their observing openness, they can feel like something is wrong with them.

The Need for the Right Environment

Because the Reflector is so fluid and variable and because of all their openness, especially their open Identity Center and their open Sacral, Reflectors must live and work in an environment that is harmonious. In a constantly changing world, Reflectors rely on their environment for stability and identity. If the environment includes a stable relationship, that will add another layer of support and ground for the Reflector but brings the additional challenge of the Reflector losing themselves in a merge with their partner. Because they reflect their immediate community, it matters who Reflectors choose for friends and partners. If your Reflector client is not surrounded by people who make them feel good, they can run into trouble with their health and wellbeing.

The Challenge of Living in a Pressure System

The open centers take in and amplify the energy around them. For the Reflectors, this means they are feeling all the energies around them, amplifying them at the same time they're trying to sort out what is theirs and what belongs to others. The

Reflector's open Head Center creates a pressure system to come up with answers while their open Root Center pressures them to take action. Their open Throat Center is under pressure to speak; their open G Center is pressed to have an identity; their open Will Center is looking to prove their value; their open Emotional and Spleen Centers are trying to navigate and manage emotions and fears. Reflectors have to learn to tolerate all the energies that constantly bombard them or else risk health issues. They have the pressing challenge of shifting to a witnessing mode rather than identifying with what they feel, think, or experience. It sounds like a lot, and what I know is that Reflectors are made for this task. To process all the world's input is their dharma.

Not Knowing When Enough Is Enough

With the open Sacral Center comes the vulnerability of not knowing when enough is enough. Like the Manifestor and Projector, the Reflector will take on and amplify the energy around them. They can appear to have great amounts of energy, the only problem is that it is not sustainable. If the Reflector is conditioned to believe they are a Generator or if they are not wise about their energy, they can burn themselves out.

The Need for Rest and to Be Out
of the Projection Field

Not having sustainable energy requires that Reflectors be mindful of getting enough rest and keep self-care in the foreground. Reflectors need time away from all Types to dissipate the energies they've encountered in the day. Nature is one of their big antidotes, and being alone in nature can be a healing salve for Reflectors. One Reflector wrote to me about her story of living in Wilderness National Parks for thirty-five years and how supreme nature is for Reflectors.

Appearing Invisible

The Reflectors shifting appearance in response to their environment can make them chameleon-like and invisible to others. This is compounded with their propensity to give up who they are to blend in or be part of their surroundings. People are generally unaccustomed to the level of reflection and mirroring Reflectors offer, and instead of realizing they are being seen tend to project onto the Reflector. Between the mix of being projected on and all their openness, Reflectors appear and often experience themselves as invisible. This is astounding on one level, as they are magnificent energetic beings in contact with the whole of life. When Reflectors are seen, they can show up full screen on the large stage of life.

Here's an example of a Reflector being invisible and being projected on while at the same time reflecting her community:

Most likely you heard the international news story of Amanda Eller who was lost in the Makawao Forest on Maui this past May for seventeen days. A few weeks after she was found, she came to me for a Human Design session. Turns out she is a Reflector.

Amanda is currently writing a book on her experience, which will reveal more about her experience of getting lost, being in the arms of nature for those seventeen days, the journey of being found, and the extraordinary efforts her family and the Maui community made to find her. You'll learn first-hand about the experience of Reflectors when you read her book. One of the things she spoke to me about was the helicopters going right over her and not seeing her. In her book, she will talk about the moment she became visible. I honestly don't think a Type with defined centers would have had that same invisibility cloak.

I live on Maui and that forest is basically in my backyard. On the first day Amanda was recognized as missing, Yarrow and I happened to go for a walk in the forest. As we drove up, we saw the crowds of people and police cars. We asked if everything was okay. Someone said, "We hope so." We came home and started watching the news. By chance, we had just been referred to Amanda for healing work and physical therapy by a close friend. Amanda's disappearance felt very personal. Like most of Maui, we were intensely engaged in the efforts to find her. News updates, posters, and videos were a daily absorption. Everywhere her disappearance was a topic of discussion and speculation. The community response was mind-blowing. People dropped everything to help find her. There was a vortex of humanity's love and care that permeated the island.

At the same time, there were so many theories and beliefs about what had happened to her including the worst-case scenarios. For my part, I couldn't feel her. My best shot was that she had been abducted. Intuitives also had difficulty locating her. Nobody could figure out what happened to her. It was as if she had disappeared into thin air. After running her chart, it all made perfect sense.

Both while she was missing and when she was found, the projections were prolific and varied. I was astounded as I watched the press and the Facebook posts cycle between the miracle of her survival and blaming and attacking her, asserting that she had somehow masterminded the whole disaster. Some people were upset with Amanda for getting lost in the first place. Everyone had an opinion. Given that Amanda is a Reflector, we can better understand the flare-up of intense feelings about her – both positive and negative – and why her story was a world-wide event. Everyone was essentially feeling themselves.

I interviewed Amanda about her experience being a Reflector for the Quantum Alignment Show. To watch the hour-long YouTube please go to: https://youtu.be/GYRMiPrH19Q

Wait for a Full Lunar Cycle
Before Making Decisions

This is the Strategy Ra advised Reflectors. It makes sense. Reflectors have all that openness and have to take time to sort out what's theirs and what's someone else's thoughts, feelings, and beliefs. I guess I'm questioning it at the moment after receiving an email from Reflector Connor Sauer who has been exploring her Reflector nature since 1997. More recently, she's been meeting with a group of Reflectors who span three generations. Questioning what's been written about them by non-Reflectors, this group is using their direct experience to discover what is true for them. One of the things they don't resonate with is the twenty-eight-day cycle, even though they understand how it was arrived at.

Disappointment

Reflectors can see what's possible for people and humanity. If things don't go as they envision, Reflectors can be deeply disappointed. Once Reflectors know who they are and how unique their design is, this deep disappointment can be partially mitigated with the understanding that not all people are like they are. The challenge for your Reflector client is to develop compassion and understanding for people who are not as flexible and capable of shifting and connecting with the infinite universe as the Reflectors are.

HOW TO APPROACH YOUR REFLECTOR CLIENT

1. Enter the mystery, honor their fluidity, and recognize their mirroring function
2. Ask them open-ended questions

3. Support your client to consider rest and environment

4. Support them to be in healthy relationships

5. Support their Strategy – take time with their decisions

6. Work with their disappointment

Respect Your Reflector's Fluidity and Recognize Their Mirroring Function

First, let me say that you will not have many Reflector clients. I have only run charts for four. As the therapist or coach, you will find yourself being seen and impacted by your Reflector client in an incredible (and sometimes an unnerving) way. It is inevitable. The same is true of everyone around the Reflector. Your self-witnessing light must be turned on even brighter with this unusual, and, in many ways, unknowable type. They are mirroring you. If you can allow yourself to be in the unknown, in the mystery with them, not needing them to be somebody you recognize consistently, that will make space for them to open to their fluidity and relieve some of the pressure to show up in a consistent way to appease your anxiety.

You have a very unique being in your care. If you are meeting rigidity or a fixed certainty, you can guess that the Reflector is not resting in their openness, and instead living out some programing or imprinting

If you are a Reflector therapist or coach, you may thrive working in partnership with another person who has sustainable energy and is more visible to the clients. With your openness, you will undoubtedly have access to a deep well of insights. The Reflectors I know are deeply intuitive and have easy access to information purely and clearly. If as a Reflector you can stay in your witness and not take people personally, your extraordinary capacities and insights will be of great benefit.

Ask Your Reflector Open-ended Questions

As far as communication goes, you will want to use the same open-ended kind of questions that all open Sacral Centers require. Stay away from *yes/no* questions that pull on the conditioning of the Sacral. You will also want to leave a lot of space for the Reflector to talk without your input or opinions so that they can hear themselves, and make decisions as they are ready. Be mindful of not pressuring them.

Support Your Reflector Client to Consider Rest and Environment

Know that your Reflector client does well with plenty of rest and needs space away from other types to regenerate. You can assume if Reflectors are not doing well that they are not in a healthy environment and must seriously consider changing locations. Think about their need to move to a healthy environment in the same way you would think about moving a plant that was getting too much or not enough water or light.

Support the Reflector to
Be in a Healthy Relationship

While Reflectors demand alone time to know themselves, they also do well being in a relationship with someone who is consistent and helps them have an internal consistency – whether it is a partnership or a friend. One Reflector client said that when she is not in a committed relationship, that a committed friend always shows up. Another Reflector I know thrives in a stable relationship with a Generator. The Generator has deep respect and trust in the Reflector and listens carefully to what the Reflector says, needs, and wants.

Support the Reflector Strategy to
Take Their Time Making Decisions

As we said before, Reflectors need to take their time making decisions. You will want to give the Reflector plenty of time (the understanding is a full moon cycle), to gather all the information they need to make decisions that feel good to them.

Our culture is generally not so patient with this process. I have watched the Reflector Ammachi, also called the Hugging Saint, be painfully slow in making decisions about the timing of her world tours. Decisions, quite frankly, that impact hotel and flight reservations and thousands of people's schedules. She can't be budged. It's almost like she's feeling into the world to gather information to decide the right timing.

On another note, because Reflectors don't have a solid sense of themselves unless they have surrendered to their Type, they may not make transitions easily and may need time to orient themselves to new surroundings, new jobs, new relationships.

Support the Reflector to Work with Their Disappointments

Reflectors understand the possibility of humanity and are working at a level to lift humanity that may be beyond our understanding. The capacity to see people's potential can leave Reflectors deeply disappointed when people fall short of who Reflectors know they can be. I think this may be one of the Reflector's heartbreaks, but this puzzle piece has no choice but to continue their mission of uniting humanity in the experience of Oneness.

FAMOUS REFLECTOR: AMMACHI

If you know anything about Ammachi, you'll know that she defies what seems humanly possible. She hugs millions of people, showering love and compassion on people around the world. You could say she lives the dharma of the Reflector. She takes in the energy of suffering and transforms it. From her awakened state, she lives in Oneness with all of life and serves to uplift humanity.

Other famous Reflectors include Rosalyn Carter, Sandra Bullock, Scott Hamilton, Fyodor Dostoyevsky, Richard Burton, and H.G. Wells.

Body

▼ 52.2 ⊙

58.2 ⊕

41.2 ♌

31.2 ℧

38.5 ☽

56.6 ☿

23.2 ♀

52.6 ♂

35.1 ♃

57.6 ♄

54.5 ⚷

53.4 ♅

32.1 ♆

▼ 4.3 ♇

Mind

⊙ 46.6

⊕ 25.6 ▲

♌ 60.6

℧ 56.6

☽ 8.6

☿ 57.4

♀ 59.4 ▲

♂ 40.3 ▼

♃ 12.4

♄ 50.1

⚷ 54.1

♅ 62.3 ▲

♆ 32.3

♇ 4.6

www.geneticmatrix.com

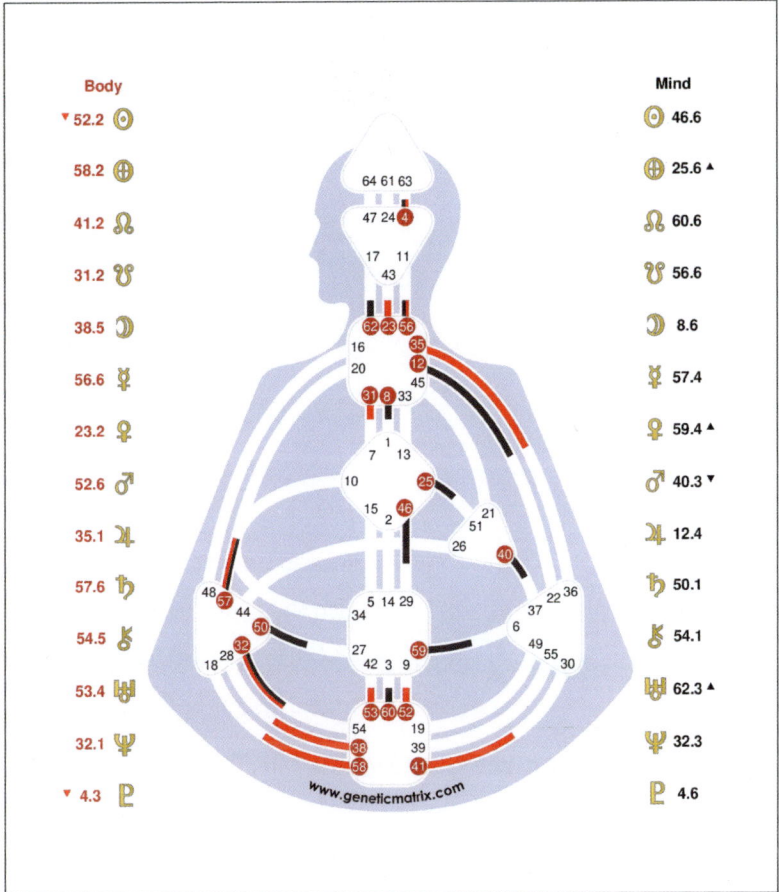

Type:	**Reflector**	Themes:	**Surprise / Disappointment**
Profile:	**6/2 - Role Model / Hermit**	Birth Date (UTC):	**27 September 1953, 03:40**
Definition:	**None**	Birth Date (Local):	**27 September 1953, 09:10**
Inner Authority:	**No Inner Authority**	Design Date (UTC):	**27 June 1953, 17:25:40**
Strategy:	**Wait a Lunar Cycle**	Birth Place:	**Parayakadavu, KL, India**
Incarnation Cross:	**LAX Healing 2**		

CHAPTER 12

THE FOUR KINDS OF AUTHORITY – HELPING YOUR CLIENTS MAKE ALIGNED DECISIONS

So far, we have been looking at Type and Strategy. The third foundational piece is Authority. This information provides potent guidance when it comes to making decisions and helping your clients make decisions.

Just to review Type and Strategy so they're fresh in your mind:

- Generators have defined Sacral Centers and no motor to the Throat Center; their Strategy is to respond
- Manifesting Generators have a defined Sacral Center and a motor to the Throat Center; their Strategy is to respond and inform
- Manifestors have an open Sacral Center and a motor to the Throat Center; their Strategy is to inform
- Projectors have an open Sacral Center and no motor to the Throat Center; their Strategy is to wait for the invitation

- Reflectors have no centers defined; their Strategy is to wait twenty-nine days before acting or making decisions

When it comes to Authority, we are looking at your client's best decision-making process. Some literature will have a more complex view on this but we will stick with 4 basic kinds of Authority or decision-making processes:

4 KINDS OF AUTHORITY

1. Emotional Authority
2. Splenic Authority
3. Sacral Authority
4. No Authority

When you look at a person's chart, you will see one of these 4 classifications of Authority noted. I suggest you look at your chart first and play with your Authority to get a sense of how this information feels to you and see if it helps you navigate the myriad of decisions you make. From that place, you can explore introducing this to your clients to support their decision-making process. Remember that the decision-making strategy (AKA the Authority) always works in tandem with the Type and Strategy. Just to be clear, in Human Design, the mind is *never* looked to for decision-making. While the mind is a great source of discernment and information, it is not in the position of guidance and direction.

Emotional Authority

At my first Human Design session, I was told I had Emotional Authority and was not designed to make spontaneous decisions. This has been an extremely helpful guide for me, and when I forget it, I inevitably regret a decision I've made, often finding myself in the awkward position of having to renege later. When you have Emotional Authority, flash sales or pressured sales are not your friends. When I signed up for The Author Incubator, there was an understanding that at the time of the interview that if I were to be accepted into the program, I would have to decide and commit at that moment, cash in hand. You could call it a pressured time frame. I was keenly aware of that and the marketing style that many programs use to illicit a commitment. I had just joined a marketing program where I had made a fairly quick decision to join (when desperation comes, it's easy to override Authority!). I would have to get out of the prior commitment if I decided to step into The Author Incubator and write this book.

The angle The Author Incubator pitched was that people who were ready to commit now were the people who would be successful in finishing their books. Those were the people they wanted in their program. Even though the pitch was to *decide now*, I was aware that I had been sitting with this decision over time. I had been following the videos Angela had produced and more than once began filling out the application for The Author Incubator program. On the day that I spontaneously completed the application, I had a solid Sacral *yes* to at least fill it out. I surprised myself. It's like I had been sitting with this possibility over time already. I intuitively felt I was a good fit, and that out of the 1,500 to 2,000 applicants I would be accepted. I knew it would mean letting the other program go which I loved and to which I had made a year-long commitment. In retrospect, I see I had already waited out my wave. It was a done deal. The pressure sales style didn't touch me and wasn't about me. It was simply time for me to write my book.

The Emotional Authority is the most complex of the 4 Authorities. If the chart has a defined Emotional Solar Plexus (the triangle on the right is colored in), then the person will have an Emotional Authority. People with Emotional Authority have consistent access to their feelings and are designed to pause before they make decisions. They must wait out their emotional wave to make sure their decision is clear. Here it gets a bit more complex, as there are 3 different kinds of emotional waves, depending on what channels connect to the Emotional Solar Plexus.

3 Kinds of Emotional Waves:
1. Individual
2. Tribal
3. Collective

The Individual Wave
If the chart has the Channels 39-55 or 22-12, the person has a wave that is designed to be deeply emotional and moody. In our culture we are taught there is something wrong if you are experiencing anything other than happy. Huge amounts of money are made on this presumption. Human Design steps in

with a different perspective. Imagine if we medicated Goethe or Rilke? People with these channels defined have consistent access to the full range of human emotion. They are designed to feel the high highs and low lows of humanity. When making a decision, they need to take their time and make sure they feel good about what they are deciding. They need to allow the full course of their wave. For each person, the length of the wave is different and that will be part of your client's exploration. If a client was low on their wave, you wouldn't want them to make a hasty decision about leaving a relationship or job, for instance. Rather, you might coach them to increase their self-care during the low wave and see what they feel as that wave shifts, what the overall feeling is. The rule of thumb is that if there is doubt, it's most likely a *no*.

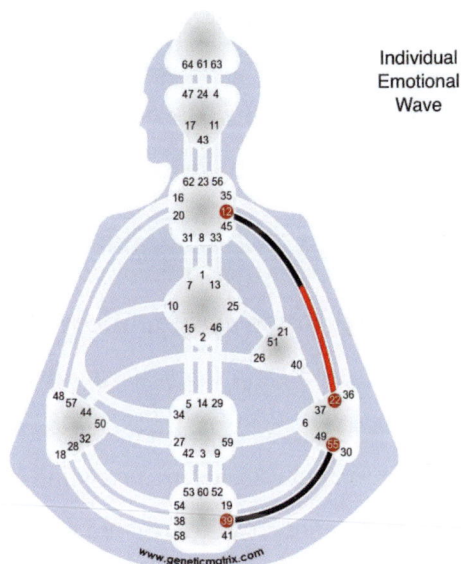

Individual Emotional Wave

www.geneticmatrix.com

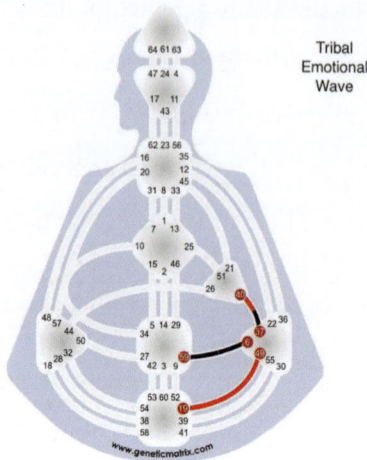

Tribal
Emotional
Wave

www.geneticmatrix.com

The Tribal Wave

If your client has the Channel 19-49, 59-6, or 37-40, they need to take into consideration a different kind of energy. Less of a wave as in highs and lows, this tribal wave is more relational. The tribal energy is passionate. It engages in sex, marriage, and war. If these kinds of decisions are made hastily, the consequences can be dire and result in anything from unwanted pregnancies to nuclear war. Tribal energy is concerned with feeding, nourishing, educating people for the survival of the tribe. It involves agreements and contracts. All of these take time and require clarity. When a tribal agreement is breached, then the consequences can be devastating. Work with your clients who have Tribal Waves to feel their passion and then take their time when making decisions. If you have a child with the Tribal Wave, make sure your agreements are clear with them. It can be heartbreaking if they are misunderstood or not honored.

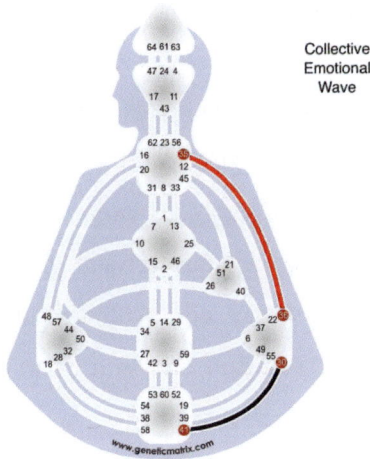

Collective
Emotional
Wave

The Collective Wave

If your client has the Channel 41-30 or 36-35, you will want to introduce them to the idea of the Collective Wave. Unlike the Individual Wave that swings from high highs to low lows, the Collective Wave builds, reaches a peak, then crashes. You may have a client who is fine one moment but then something is said or comes into the field and they lose it. This is the Collective Wave at work. Like the Individual Wave, it will take time and exploration for your client to understand and work with their Collective Wave.

Multiple Waves

Yes, your client can have more than one kind of wave. In this case, they will need to respect each wave. Again, this is a process of exploration, learning to know oneself.

I've watched clients who've mastered knowing their waves be more responsible to themselves and make grounded decisions that weren't available to them when they thought they were supposed to follow their gut or their heart in the heat of the moment. I've watched Karen Curry Parker modify her marketing to make space for those of us who need time to make sustainable decisions. Too many times she has had students with Emotional Authority sign up for courses then back out.

Splenic Authority

The Spleen Center is the center of intuition in the moment. I like to call it the whispering center because its voice can be missed if you're not listening closely to your guidance. Your clients with Splenic Authority will need to explore how they hear their guidance and how they recognize the information. Perhaps it is a voice, a felt sensation, or a knowing. Some say the intuition only speaks once, and if you don't pay attention, it will be lost. Others say when it knocks three times they know it is true. The thing to remember is that the spleen is *in the now*; the guidance can change and therefore there is the need to keep listening as circumstances change.

Sacral Authority

Like it sounds, the Sacral Authority is connected to the Sacral Center – that motor that has a binary response: on/off or *yes/no*. When your client has Sacral Authority, they are designed to be spontaneous and make decisions according to their Sacral response. "Do you want to go to the movies?" "*Yes*." People with a Sacral Authority can trust their guidance in the moment. Now, that Sacral response can change if new information or expanded information comes into the field. Your partner asks if you want to go to the movies, you get a *yes*, then they tell you they're going to a horror flick. You may still get a *yes*, or you may get a *no*. Again, with all the authorities, it is a matter of exploring and getting clear how your authority functions and when to check again. As you might imagine, Manifestors, Projectors, and Reflectors will not have Sacral Authority.

No Authority

When your client has No Authority, they have the tricky task of finding people (hopefully you are one of them) who can be clear, non-biased listeners to share their thoughts with. As those with No Authority hear themselves, they can know what they think/feel and the right course of action. I have a Projector client who, before I knew Human Design, my approach was to be quite active in guiding her and "supporting" her. What I didn't realize was that I was seeing her through my Generator lens, believing that she should be acting in ways I knew to be effective – like a Generator. Not only that, but I was sure I was her wise guide. That's what she was paying me for, right? Once I got clear first about her being a Projector, and then that she had No Authority, I retrained myself to listen deeply to her, giving her space to hear herself. It's been a very powerful and empowering lesson for both of us. All Reflectors have No Authority. If you know you are with a Reflector, you would do well to stop any inclination to offer input and become all-ears.

Now that you have learned about your clients' Type, Strategy, and Authority and have begun to work with them from this vantage, you're ready to see what lies ahead in terms of obstacles you might encounter and the next level of learning Human Design that awaits you.

Section 4

Going Forward

CHAPTER 13

MAKING YOUR WAY

We're coming to the end of this portion of our journey together. You've been introduced to a lot of information. You've learned the fundamentals of Human Design. You now know how Human Design came into being and what its origins are. You can look at a chart at a basic level and recognize what's conscious, what's unconscious, what hexagrams the planets are in, and how to transpose the hexagrams onto the bodygraph. You're familiar with the 9 Centers, and the difference between Channels and Hanging Gates. You understand how to tell what's defined, what's open, and what that means. Hopefully, by this time you can tell what Type someone is by looking at the chart. You have a clear understanding of the different Types and their Strategies: Generator (wait to respond), Manifesting Generator (wait to respond and inform), Manifestor (inform before taking action), Projector (wait to be invited or acknowledged), and Reflector (wait a full moon cycle before making decisions). You're schooled in each Type's gifts, challenges, and ways to approach them. You've learned about Authority and its support in the decision-making process. You've run your chart, your family's, friends', and colleagues' charts, and perhaps even started running your clients' charts. You've stepped into the waters of Human Design. You're ready to use Human Design as a tool in your work.

Maybe the information was a bit much to digest. Maybe you need more support in having it land and becoming facile with it. Maybe reading about it is not your best way to receive the transmission. That's totally reasonable. We all have different learning styles. You may need to work with someone in person to talk it through and use examples of people you know in a more hands-on way to have it make sense.

In any event, once you are ready to take Human Design into your work, there are some things you may encounter as you go forward.

CHALLENGES WITH INCORPORATING HUMAN DESIGN

My friend Tammy is the CEO of a large nonprofit. We met in the Transformational Speaking training when we were randomly partnered. Tammy has a powerful story to tell and is here to empower people. She works with her team using various profiling systems to help people know themselves and work more effectively. Her vision is to create a forum to support women in leadership. When Tammy found out I did Human Design, she jumped at the opportunity to have her chart read. She was profoundly moved by the reflection she received and came away from the session wanting to learn more. She saw how incredible it would be to bring Human Design to her work. In the few months while I was writing this book, she was exploring Human Design. When we spoke recently, it was clear that it was confusing to her what she had to know and how much she had to know before she could use the system effectively. Her question thrilled me because she was touching on exactly why I wrote this book. My passion is helping professionals bring Human Design into their work in a user-friendly way.

Too Much Information!

Tammy's first challenge was sorting through the information on Human Design and discerning what to use and how to use it.

I am hoping that it's clear in this book that your first task is to immerse yourself in learning about the 5 Types, their Strategies, and the 4 Authorities, then begin using this information in a lived way with your clients or team members. Applying the Types, Strategy, and Authority is a foundational practice, similar to foundational meditation practices in Tibetan Buddhism. You have to apply the knowledge. Be open to discovering who your clients are through their Type. If you've got it and can do it on your own, great. If you need support to work with the material and integrate more deeply, either one-on-one consulting or a group supervision setting can be supportive in the process of becoming skillful. The important thing is to move your understanding off the shelf and into action as a practice. Remember, you are asking yourself to open to a right-brain download. You are asking yourself to receive information that is new and unfamiliar to our brains and bring it to your clients. Take your time. Trust the process.

At this point in your journey, it can be tempting to gobble up the whole meal of Human Design. I would be cautious about bringing in too much Human Design information without first putting the basics into practice. There are a few reasons for this. One, it can be compelling to stay at the intellectual level and learn *about* Human Design. The second reason is that, like Tammy, you can get overwhelmed by the bounty of information that can initially be quite hard to grok. You may feel like you need to know it all before you can use it. I advise against that tact as there are layers and layers of information that take time to understand and integrate.

Not only that, but choosing from the many streams of Human Design can be confusing in and of itself. There are many different approaches to Human Design. One way to think of it is to look at the variety of Christian churches from Unitarian to Fundamentalist, Catholic to Protestant. Each takes the teachings of Jesus and interprets them through their particular lens. Some have a wrathful God, others a loving God. Or if you're Buddhist, the teachings of the Buddha have been transmitted through several lineages over time. Some lineages focus on accessing the teachings through study, others through meditation practice. Different streams focus on different aspects of the teachings. Likewise, Human Design has many different streams of interpretation and understanding. Some are profoundly esoteric and some more user-friendly.

The stream that spoke to me and resonates with my sensibilities is the one I've spent seven years learning with Karen Curry Parker. She worked closely with Ra, and his message to her was clear: he did not own the information; it came through him but belongs to everyone. Karen believes that Human Design needs to be available to as many people as possible. She has a simple, easy approach that is deeply respectful and loving. It is from that stream that I work and play with Human Design, bringing it to coaches, therapists, and business owners.

Convincing People to Use the System

The next question Tammy asked was, "How do you get people to use the system?" She was concerned that people wouldn't be open to a system that relied on birth time. Maybe Human Design was too out there. I think that's a valid question. Human Design is new and unfamiliar. As it becomes more known, I believe that will be less of an issue. I can remember doing yoga in 1976 when people thought it was a weird, esoteric practice. Now it's entered the mainstream. Already, more and more transformational businesses are talking about and learning about Human Design. I think it will soon approach that hundredth monkey point where it will be recognized as the breakthrough tool that it is, and integrated into the mainstream.

I can remember the first couples therapist Yarrow and I went to in the early 80s. She was an intern at JFK University and had asked for our birth information before our first session because she wanted to look at our astrology to help understand us. That was definitely outside the frame of the work I'd done with other therapists. I don't remember therapy with her as life-changing, but I do remember she ran our charts.

Depending on who you are and what you're working on, it may not be feasible to use Human Design with all of your clients. You're going to have to be comfortable asking your clients for their birth information. That may be too out-of-the-box for some of your clients unless you can articulate the system in a way that engages their curiosity. You have to have enough experience with Human Design that you know the power of it.

I've worked with some clients who I wouldn't have expected to be open to Human Design, but their trust in me enabled them to check it out. Sometimes people with a lot of logic in their charts or with very little definition in the Individual Channels will be skeptical. I have a brother who got his MBA from Harvard Business School, a big CEO guy, who tends to relish his skeptical view. I was running charts at a family reunion and he reluctantly let me look at his. As I was describing his chart and one of his Projector children's charts he remarked how uncannily accurate they appeared to be. This is the response I find over and over. People are surprised at the accuracy.

At this point whenever I work with someone new, I tell them in the initial call that I use Human Design as an assessment tool to support me in my work with them. I explain that I will need their birth information if we are going to work together. I wouldn't think of not having their chart available for our work.

Challenges with Birth Time

Which brings us to challenges with the birth time. In chapter 3, I spoke a bit about this. I'll just reiterate here that if your client does want to explore their chart with you but they don't have their birth time, you have a few choices:

1. You can have them ask their parents for a ballpark time or have them check with the hospital where they were born for their birth certificate. If the birth time is not on the birth certificate, there is a chance the local county records department has the time recorded.

2. If you have a ballpark time, you can run charts around that time and see if the chart changes. An easy way to tell is if the profile numbers change (this is marked on the chart) or if the moon sign changes.

3. If they don't have a ballpark time and you like this sort of thing (I do!), you can go through the day running charts every two hours to see if the chart changes.

4. You can hire someone to do a time rectification for you. This could be a Human Design specialist or an astrologer. I spend so much time on this because it's essential to have the right chart.

On that note, I have made the error on more than one occasion of inputting the wrong birth information and reading an inaccurate chart. It's very humbling and just plain wrong. Now I make a point to ask the client to double-check the birth information before sharing their chart with them. Just recently I skipped this step when I had some new friends over for dinner. In my enthusiasm, I ran my friend's chart and gave her an at-the-dinner-table mini-reading. One of the things I said didn't resonate. I found myself trying to override her experience (bad practice!). Later, I discovered that I had inputted her birth information incorrectly.

Another option that bypasses your human error is to have your clients run their chart at freehumandesignchart.com and email it or bring it to you.

FORGING AHEAD

We've covered Type, Strategy, and Authority, which is the foundational ground of Human Design. We typically say in a Human Design session that if the client gets those three things, that is enough. That lays the path for a new journey of self-discovery. From here, you will be working with your client to help them use these guides to navigate their lives more successfully.

As you become comfortable working with Type, Strategy, and Authority with your clients, you may get the Human Design bug and be drawn to go deeper into the bodygraph to enrich your work. When you are ready, there are layers of information to add in and bring more depth to your understanding of yourself and your clients. I look forward to sharing that with you when the time is right!

CHAPTER 14

A PARADIGM SHIFT

"You are not a problem to be solved."
– Pali Summerlin

I don't know if you've heard of John Sarno. I was recently introduced to his work by Pali Summerlin when I was suffering from back pain. In the 1980s, John Sarno was an MD treating people with back pain. After seeing the lack of success through surgery, he concluded that we were looking at the situation from the wrong vantage and, as a result, drawing inaccurate conclusions. In the majority of cases, the back pain is not, he believed, caused by a structural or muscular disorder (discs, etc.). Nor is inflammation the source. Thus surgery, bed rest, and anti-inflammatories are not the solution. He takes the radical stand that there is nothing wrong at the physical level. The problem, the pain, he concludes, is a lack of oxygen caused by muscles contracting in response to repressed emotional distress. He explains that people used to get ulcers until it was determined that they were caused by psychological stress, at which point they became less attractive. Now, when people can't process something or don't want to feel something, they put it behind them, literally in their backs. The result is tension, causing a lack of oxygen, resulting in pain. Dr. Sarno's highly effective program involved getting people's minds onboard with the idea that there was nothing wrong with their backs but that they needed to let go of the beliefs that something was wrong and work through the psychological issues. His success was astounding. People who had been in wheelchairs and bed-ridden were given new lives. People with long-standing back pain had a way to actually work with themselves and to feel when they were putting something behind them and clear it up immediately.

What if, for a moment, we think of Human Design in this light: that our clients (and ourselves!) have taken on a story or a belief that they're in pain and limitation because there is a fundamental problem – something is wrong with them? What if all that is happening is a misunderstanding that is causing the constriction of our vital force? A mistaken identity. If we think we should be different than we are, we suffer. If your clients are in a room and they can't perceive a door, they will feel trapped or disempowered. Knowing their design helps them differen-tiate; it shows them the door. Imagine a Projector who thinks something is wrong with them because they're not being heard, and then they learn that they aren't designed to be heard unless they're invited or acknowledged. Can you feel how the stigma falls away? The shift in identity?

On the other hand, as the practitioner, you can be part of the limitation. Like the orthopedic surgeon who declares something is wrong and calls for back surgery, you can collude with the belief that someone is deficient because they're struggling to be heard, and you can engage in the spin to solve the problem: "Maybe it was your mother," or "Maybe you need to do more affirmations." The belief that there is a problem is solidified. Everyone is in agreement that something is wrong. All our tools are great and helpful, but the opportunity here is a shift from solving the problem to seeing that people fundamentally aren't broken and don't need fixing. When you can differentiate who the person is, it takes away the assumption that they are a victim or that the people around them are disempowering them. It shifts the agency to the client. Honestly, it makes your work much easier.

We are looking to shift the paradigm from what is the problem that needs to be solved and what is the deficiency that needs to be addressed to what's your client's piece and are they aligning with that or living that – or not. My hope is that you begin to see your clients with clear eyes, that you detach (and help them detach) from their stories, that you see their operating system, and support them in getting back online with themselves.

Let me give you an example from my own life.

I was the first girl after five boys, followed by a sister almost five years later. My dad, as I've mentioned, was a cardiovascular surgeon, yet it was Mom who was the powerhouse. She got her pilot's license in her late forties, flew cross country in the women's Powderpuff Derby air races, became Woman Pilot of the Year, and eventually was in the Women Pilots' Hall of Fame. She was not a snugly, cozy mom. She wasn't nurturing in the way I felt she should have been. I lived a story that I was unmothered. Let's just say I had a very well-established "mother wound" that I spent years in therapy exploring. My problem was my mother (and, I could throw in, my five older brothers). It wasn't until I was almost forty that I met Byron Katie and a piece of that story took a major hit. "My mom should be different. Is it true?" That inquiry opened one of those hidden doors that let me out of that trap. I still remember the moment it dawned on me: "Ah, she should be exactly how she is. I should be different. I want her to be nurturing. I should be nurturing her, rather than shutting her out." This was a major relief and created a dramatic shift in my life. If we return to the back analogy for a moment, I let go of a chunk of tension I was carrying, an untrue story that was limiting me and causing me pain.

It was after my mother had crossed over that I became immersed in Human Design. I ran her chart and my heart cracked open. A Manifestor. She was designed to be powerful and independent with a repelling aura. As sweet as her Southern persona was, we always knew who the boss was. As I said earlier, even my five brothers together didn't have a chance coming up against her. My mother was living her design. I thought she should be different. I suffered. I also thought I should be more like her, able to impact people, have my voice heard. My chart is different. I lost out in two ways: my story cost me my love and for her and also my love and acceptance of myself. Not that it should have been different; each part of this wounding has been essential on my path, bringing me closer to myself. But I do wonder how I would have been with her if I had known she was a Manifestor while she was alive...

Originally, in writing this book for therapists and coaches, I was thinking in terms of my dad and continuing education. I wanted this incredible technology to be available mainstream, in the same way that CT scans, MRI's, and laser surgery have become part of the norm. But as I come to the end of this book, another piece calls to be named. Drawing once more on my Tibetan Buddhist roots, I want to speak to something called termas. Termas are teachings that have been hidden away until humanity is ready to receive them. They are revealed at certain times throughout history. Even more than a tool, I believe Human Design is a terma that was revealed to Ra in that cabin off the coast of Spain in 1987. It's an information system that was offered to help us rest in who we are on our human journey as we forge forward on our evolutionary path.

We know in physics that the observer impacts what is observed. How are we observing our clients? Are we looking for problems to solve? Are we seeing the person in front of us as an ego identity that needs upgrading? There is a time and a place for all of that. In my story, part of what I had to go through was developing a healthy ego so I could begin to let go of identifying with my ego. There is a time and a place to support people in developing a working identity, a brand. But what waits beyond that is so much more.

Human Design offers a new way of looking at people, starting with the assumption that your clients are not broken, they're just not living their design. As your clients relax into their design, as they embrace it, they can initially ground on their unique definition, the energy that is consistently available to them. They begin to explore what Karen Curry Parker calls "the spectrum of potential expressions."

When I take on a new Vajrayana meditation practice, I don't understand it at first. It's pretty much always overwhelming. But as I stick with it, the practices come alive. They start speaking to me, revealing insights and opening me to new dimensions. This has been my experience with Human Design.

I engage in Human Design as a path or practice, much like the Vajrayana meditation practices. Over time, I work with my clients to become skillful with their design. They begin with their basic design: their Type, Strategy, and Authority. As they get some traction with that, we engage in the process of deconditioning or seeing where they have been attaching to mistaken identity. Inquiring into their open centers, they begin the exploration of knowing themselves as nothing and everything. Or, as the awakened Indian mystic Nisargadatta said:

"When I look inside and see that I am nothing, that is wisdom. When I look outside and see that I am everything, that is love. And between these two, my life turns."

Here we begin to approach the Truth of who we are: Awake Awareness. That is the ultimate healing, the path of liberation. The attachment to personhood as we know it has the possibility of falling away. Ultimately, we are not our design, and we cannot escape our design any more than we are our bodies nor can escape our bodies. Our design and our bodies are supports. The potential is to live in stable awareness, free of attachment to identity with no external person, place, or thing as the source of our happiness. As we see our core wounding for what it is, an essential abandonment of our self, we have the possibility of liberating ourselves.

In my life, Human Design has called on me to stabilize the distorted thinking that creates so much division and suffering. Human Design reminds me of the necessary and empowering role of diversity in the scheme of Oneness. From a Human Design perspective, each of us, perfectly designed, with an intrinsic role to play in the evolution of humanity, comes together to create one whole, a giant 8-billion-piece puzzle. It is when we allow ourselves to be true to our design that we make our greatest contribution. Likewise, when we are trying to be someone we are not we miss the opportunity to bring forth our gifts, serve humanity, and fulfill our life purpose. Bonnie Ware says one of the five greatest regrets people have on their death beds is: "I wish I had the courage to live a life true to myself, not the life others expected of me." Do not support your clients to go to their grave with this regret!

These days, when I find myself having difficulty with someone, I look at their Human Design chart. Each time, I am flooded with compassion, appreciation, and a sense of honor for who they are – their strengths and their struggles. My mind widens and makes space for their story, their unique configuration. I open to the possibility of who they are without conditioning. I also look at their chart in relation to mine. Perhaps our charts form an electromagnetic pattern that creates a challenge for us that simply *is*; not personal, just reality. Or perhaps they have a profile that has a fixed quality that calls on me to be more flexible. Maybe one of us is challenging the other with our Individual, Tribal, or Collective nature.

I remember that we are human beings – not human doings – and that each of us is finding our way. Our differences become critically important, sometimes acting as the grain of sand that creates the pearl, at other times interfacing in the electro-magnetic web to help each other to create and function in the world. We need one another on this path of evolutionary awakening. The practice of understanding and embracing diversity on the path of Oneness is a big conversation with many facets. It's a timely conversation that has huge ramifications politically, in our relationships, and even in regards to our body. My wish is that this stream of words carries the awakened transmission, showering blessings on you and your clients. May you all thrive, living lives true to yourselves.

ILLUSTRATION INDEX

ACKNOWLEDGMENTS

My first wave of gratitude is for Mama Maui. Your deep quiet, your gentle beauty, your aloha spirit embraces me as I write this book. How grateful I am to be in your arms, out of the psychic bombardment of the Mainland. How much easier it is to hear the whispers wanting a voice. Bowing to your magnificent grace I give thanks.

Angela Lauria – You are an extraordinary guide. Gifted beyond measure. Razor-sharp. Brilliant. Adorable. Unabashedly authentic and unexpectedly delightful. Your Truth detector is highly calibrated, and you aren't afraid to speak what you see. I have been called out by you and empowered by you. Thank you doesn't begin to convey the gift you've given. It's that teach a person to fish kind of gift … it keeps giving…

You, your program (The Author Incubator), and your staff have ferried me across waters I have been wanting to cross for about fifty years … your faith and trust in me allowed me to make the trip. Your commitment to love at all costs is shattering in the best of ways. Thank you.

I was nine years old, clear in my choice to be a writer when I grew up. My mom's response when I told her: "Oh, Honey, you don't want to do that. Writers don't make any money." Her words deflated me but didn't dissuade me from writing heartfelt poetry and endless volumes of journals. Books were my friends and writing was my language. After getting my BA in English Literature at UC Berkeley, I spent thirty years planning my book: Tools for Transformation. I made extensive outlines, revising them every time I got a new tool. I knew that someday... it would be time. Then, in my early forties, a well-known astrologer told me, "It's not a matter of if you publish, it's a matter of when." At sixty-one, it was time. In a one year numerologically, Angela's program kept showing up on my computer, beckoning me. On my application when she asked who had referred me My answer was "God."

Each step of the way in The Author Incubator process, I felt outrageously held and supported. Being interviewed by Heather Russell was like a spiritual experience. Watching the welcome video, I was almost pinching myself – could this be true?

The creativity temple was the clincher. I knew I was in the right hands to give birth to this dream. Then came the coaching calls – fierce love, not for the faint of heart – the no-nonsense kind of love a mother cat has when she picks up her wandering kitten by the neck and brings her back to the safety of the nest. Then Ora North, my developmental editor, stuck with me even when I was sure I knew "more better" than she. Rest assured, she was not going to let my ego have the upper hand!

I am so blessed to have the skillful eye and kind enthusiastic heart of my Projector editor Moriah Howell. Thank you for putting up with me and bringing such crystal clear guidance. This book would not be what it is without your touch. Any colloquialisms that do not adhere to standard editing protocols are at my insistence and not a reflection of Moriah's editing capacity or integrity!

Gratitude to Jeff Poole for tipping me off about the Quill so I had plenty of time to sort through my feelings and wait out my emotional wave. To Sara's Shisler Goff, a bright light walking the path before me, trusting I could do it, making it high play, I'm thoroughly enjoying the bourgeoning friendship with you and our wives. What extraordinary adventures lie ahead for us?

And to Ramses, your tender, loving coaching, and your open availability softened the hard knocks and allowed me to take a fresh look at what was really going on. To the Facebook group, my cohort, you were big teachers and great companions on this path. Who knew how much fun it would be to watch each other's progress, trials, tribulations? Cheering each other on, learning from each other was integral to my success. I'm pretty sure your voices will be there as I write in the future!

This writing journey was high-octane Love. An exercise in getting the Ego out of the way so the mystery had a chance to come through. Thank you, again, Angela for doing what you do, for standing your high ground.

In terms of Human Design, I would like to acknowledge the Light Beings that transmitted this terma, this practice, this breakthrough technology. Thank you for your generosity and tenacity, for making sure Ra got the information we needed. And thank you Ra, for being willing, reluctant as you may have been, to be the initial recipient of this knowledge and doing what it took to transmit the teachings of Human Design. Thank you also Kamud for ushering me in to this wild world of Human Design!

Heartfelt gratitude to Karen Curry Parker and her book *Understanding Human Design* that made this revolutionary information easily accessible to me and thousands of others. Thank you for your years of classes, downloading a clear stream of knowledge in an articulate, gentle and loving way. Your conviction that Human Design belongs to all of us, trusting its aliveness in us, and your deep love and support for your students and humanity is almost unfathomable. You are a shining star. Your superpower elixir is being an endless geyser of generosity, kindness, and revolutionary knowledge. I am so blessed to hold my cup at your fountain.

To the Guides who bless my journey, pointing the way, over and over and over again… my heart alchemically bursts into a cosmic embrace when I think of you. I owe my life as I know it to you: Byron Katie, Tara, Amma, Lama Palden, Ram Dass, Faisal Muqaddam, Leslie Temple Thurston, Karen Seager, Ellen Zucker, Anat Baniel, Ming Tong Gu, Barbara Kaufman, Eileen

Poole, Charlene Tschirhart, Vicki Noble, Marion Rosen, Karen Curry Parker, and the eighty-year-old jewel inhabiting in the temple below me, Pali Summerlin.

Thank you, Stephanie Brill, for knowing I would someday land on Maui, and for your Aloha extending to us when the time was right.

To the clients who have walked the path with me, I am honored by your trust. Some of you began with me when I was a Rosen Method Bodywork practitioner back in the late 80s. Every time I learned something new, you got it. We kept upgrading together: feminist psychology, Holographic Repatterning, The Work of Byron Katie, Squares, Releasing, The Diamond Approach, Tibetan Buddhist teachings, Neuro-Movement, Human Design … just to name a few. I have the deepest respect for all of you. Thank you for rolling with me. Thank you for your commitment to yourselves. Thank you for risking knowing yourSelf. My heart belongs to you.

It takes a village, and I most certainly would not be who I am or where I am without the support and companionship of my deep, wild and wonderful beloved friends: Jane and Gary Bell, Pearlyn Goodman-Herrick, Arina Isaacson, Sandy Wallenstein, The Pearls: Debra Chamberlin-Taylor, Toni Littlejohn, Clare McLaughlin, Devi Weisenburg, Gwen Gordon, Julie Wester, (and Yarrow). My Maui companions: The PL8's: Rae Ariel, Judy Gabriel, Zelie Duvauchelle, Lucia Maya, Lee Stein, Cynthia Cary (and Yarrow). Jeanette Van Horn and Andrew Zehr,

Sue Perley (your sweet hale was a life saver!), Ane and Marc Takaha, the Ram Dass hui. And to all of you unnamed, who have and continue to touch my life, thank you.

Also, my heartfelt gratitude to Karla Downing and Alive Retreats – your love and trust in me and what I have to offer is wind beneath my wings. The Sukhasiddhi sangha, especially my Lineage family – this journey we've walked together has allowed me to understand the Human Design chart in a profound and transformational way. Thank you for your companionship on the path.

A deep mahalo to the facilitators, staff and women who attended the Women Within Weekend held on Maui in April. Something very magical happened during my carpet work where an internal switch was flipped that enabled me to step out into the world in May and step into this book writing process.

I can see my parents, my grandparents, and my nephew Finn cheering from the other side. We're all shaking our heads while we smile ear to ear – at once in disbelief that I finally wrote something, at the same time thoroughly enjoying the display. Bravo they shout! As I come around the homestretch.

Meanwhile, my extraordinary siblings: my five older brothers, Pete, David, Michael, Steven, and Christopher, and my younger sister, Heidi, have inspired me with their unusual paths into uncharted waters. The spirit that anything is possible is the message our tribe conveys. Maybe it comes with the Winn name? Heidi, my soul sister, I love you. You have always been my biggest fan, recognizing, embodying and sharing the wisdom that comes through me. You and Jean rock! I'm handing you over to Angela to midwife your book. It's time for you to step into your big shoes!

My eyes brimming with tears of awe, I thank you, Yarrow, my beloved wife. For thirty-eight years you have beat to your own drum. Your Projector nature refusing to be hijacked by my Generator ways has taught me about the value of connection, pleasure, possibility, and living out of the box. How we – me as a dog and you as a cat – have found our way through the myriad challenges we've faced is, in and of itself, miraculous. That our journey together has been one of awakening to the Truth of who we are is Grace. You are the best high play companion! Thank you for being the moon. Thank you for your unending support. Thank you for being you.

Final thanks goes to my Inner author who dared to speak in the face of fear. Who braved my open throat, open G, open head, open ajna, open will, Gate 63, my superego attacks, my terror of being seen. You chose to step out into the light with your brilliance. I love your quirky tenacity. I love your conviction that you have words waiting to be spoken and heard. I love your insistence, that whatever the cost, it's time.

THANK YOU

Thank you –

For diving into these waters with me. For seeing or sensing that this tool, the Human Design System was a light switch you wanted to turn on. For not being afraid of what you might discover. For opening your hearts and minds to the journey of awakening to the truth of who you and your clients are. For being one of the guides that are here to selflessly support others on the path to discovering and embracing who they are.

May Human Design be a light to guide you in your life and in your work. May you use this knowledge wisely. May you and your work be showered with blessings.

In gratitude I am offering a surprise free gift. Please contact me at info@clientsandhumandesign.com to collect.

Are you moved by this work? Do you want to deepen your knowledge and skill in using Human Design with clients? Would you like a Human Design Consultation for yourself or supervision for one of your clients? Do you run a transformational program and understand how valuable it is for your staff and/or participants to work with their design. Would you like consultation with your program?

Contact me: info@clientsandhumandesign.com

Looking forward to hearing how your adventure with Human Design transforms your life and the lives of your clients!

Blessings,

Robin

P.S. If you have *any* niggling to write *your* book… go for it. If you need help/support, check out The Author Incubator. If it's a fit, you're lucky indeed!

Robin Winn has integrated her innovative system with hundreds of therapists and coaches to shift the dynamic of communications and the understanding of differences in families, partnerships, and teams. Teenagers are seen, couples shift from judging to respecting, and business owners have clear guidance to support team member's strengths.

Robin has B.A. in English Literature from UC Berkeley, and an M.A. in Feminist Psychology from New College. Her extensive experience as a licensed therapist, somatic practitioner,

Diamond Logos teacher, dharma leader and Human Design Coach enable her to shed light on a vast array of challenges from a wide perspective.

Robin lives on Maui with her wife of 38 years.

DP

DIFFERENCE
PRESS

ABOUT DIFFERENCE PRESS

Difference Press is the exclusive publishing arm of The Author Incubator, an educational company for entrepreneurs – including life coaches, healers, consultants, and community leaders – looking for a comprehensive solution to get their books written, published, and promoted. Its founder, Dr. Angela Lauria, has been bringing to life the literary ventures of hundreds of authors-in-transformation since 1994.

A boutique-style self-publishing service for clients of The Author Incubator, Difference Press boasts a fair and easy-to-understand profit structure, low-priced author copies, and author-friendly contract terms. Most importantly, all of our #incubatedauthors maintain ownership of their copyright at all times.

LET'S START A MOVEMENT WITH YOUR MESSAGE

In a market where hundreds of thousands of books are published every year and are never heard from again, The Author Incubator is different. Not only do all Difference Press books reach Amazon bestseller status, but all of our authors are actively changing lives and making a difference.

Since launching in 2013, we've served over 500 authors who came to us with an idea for a book and were able to write it and get it self-published in less than 6 months. In addition, more than 100 of those books were picked up by traditional publishers and are now available in bookstores. We do this by selecting the highest quality and highest potential applicants for our future programs.

Our program doesn't only teach you how to write a book – our team of coaches, developmental editors, copy editors, art directors, and marketing experts incubate you from having a book idea to being a published, bestselling author, ensuring that the book you create can actually make a difference in the world. Then we give you the training you need to use your book to make the difference in the world, or to create a business out of serving your readers.

ARE YOU READY TO MAKE A DIFFERENCE?

You've seen other people make a difference with a book. Now it's your turn. If you are ready to stop watching and start taking massive action, go to http://theauthorincubator.com/apply/.

"Yes, I'm ready!"

OTHER BOOKS BY DIFFERENCE PRESS

Going Home: Saying Goodbye with Grace and Joy When You Know Your Time is Short by Michael G. Giovanni Jr.

Get Happier, Fitter, and off the Meds Now: 7 Steps to Improved Health and a Body You Love by Ell Graniel

Healed: A Divinely Inspired Path to Healing Cancer by Pamela Herzer, M.A.

Live Healthy with Hashimoto's Disease: The Natural Ayurvedic Approach to Managing Your Autoimmune Disorder by Vikki Hibberd

I Left My Toxic Relationship – Now What?: The Step-by-Step Guide to Starting over and Living on Your Own by Heather J. Kent

Sign Up Your First Coaching Client: Steps to Launch Your New Career by Carine Kindinger

Find Your Beloved: Your Guide to Attract True Love by Rosine Kushnick

*My Toddler Has Stopped Having so Many Tantrums:
The Mother's Guide to Finding Joy in Parenting*
by Susan Jungermann

*In the Eye of a Relationship Storm: Know What to Do
in an Abusive Situation* by Jackquiline Ann

*My Clothes Fit Again!: The Overworked Women's Guide to
Losing Weight* by Sue Seal

How Do I Survive?: 7 Steps to Living after Child Loss
by Patricia Sheveland

Your Life Matters!: Learn to Write Your Memoir in 8 Easy Steps
by Junie Swadron

Medication Detox: How to Live Your Best Health, Simplified
by Rachel Reinhart Taylor M.D.

Keeping Well: An Anti-Cancer Guide to Remain in Remission
by Brittany Wisniewski

Printed in Great Britain
by Amazon

55733304R00162